T0072373

NAKED TRUTH
MY JOURNEY TO DIVINE INTIMACY

INELY C. CESNA

BALBOA.PRESS
A DIVISION OF HAY HOUSE

Balboa Press books may be ordered through booksellers or by contacting:

Balboa Press
A Division of Hay House
1663 Liberty Drive
Bloomington, IN 47403
www.balboapress.com
844-682-1282

Because of the dynamic nature of the Internet, any web addresses or
links contained in this book may have changed since publication and
may no longer be valid. The views expressed in this work are solely those
of the author and do not necessarily reflect the views of the publisher,
and the publisher hereby disclaims any responsibility for them.

The author of this book does not dispense medical advice or prescribe the
use of any technique as a form of treatment for physical, emotional, or medical
problems without the advice of a physician, either directly or indirectly. The
intent of the author is only to offer information of a general nature to help you
in your quest for emotional and spiritual well-being. In the event you use any
of the information in this book for yourself, which is your constitutional right,
the author and the publisher assume no responsibility for your actions.

Any people depicted in stock imagery provided by Getty Images are
models, and such images are being used for illustrative purposes only.
Certain stock imagery © Getty Images.

Print information available on the last page.

ISBN: 979-8-7652-2502-8 (sc)
ISBN: 979-8-7652-2503-5 (e)

Balboa Press rev. date: 03/23/2022

I dedicate this book to my beloved children, Katlyn and Koady, and all children in the world, young and old, so that we may honor all of who we are, embracing all parts of ourselves and growing with grace and awareness of the pure essence of love that we have always been.

TABLE OF CONTENTS

FOREWORD

My early childhood lives in memories of an immense sense of oneness with life, which I refer to as 'Divine Intimacy.' I clearly remember it as a sense of fulfillment, joy, gratitude, and pleasure where time did not seem to exist. Wonderment and enjoyment filled the whole of me, and time seemed inexistent.

I enjoyed spending entire days in the company of dogs: our family dogs and other relatives' dogs. I would walk with them in the garden, sleep in their dog houses, and lie on the ground with them. Their warm fur comforted me. Their heartbeat and their breath entertained me. I felt like we were having a deep conversation without saying a word.

I also adored the collection of rolly-pollies I gathered from the garden in front of our house. They were interesting to me because they were capable of transforming themselves right in front of my very eyes. The moment I touched them, they turned into a ball, as if they were asking me to play with them. So I would place them in my plastic bucket and keep them as toys.

My favorite aunt showed up in our house on a particular Easter afternoon with three ducklings: for me, my sister, and my brother. I enjoyed caring for them swimming with them in our inflatable pool, feeding them, and taking long walks with them in our small backyard.

Animals brought me a great sense of Divine Intimacy, just like plants. So I learned from my aunt to care for plants. Soon enough, I had many small vases of fern sitting on the kitchen window sill, which I observed as they grew and flourished.

Another one of my utter fascinations was the night sky. It overwhelmed me with profound mystery, curiosity, the feeling of oneness, and Divine Intimacy. It was factual evidence of something far beyond comprehension. I enjoyed spending hours wondering what it would be like on that side of the universe. As a child, I wanted to become an astronaut to meet my wonder face-to-face.

By the age of ten, most of my childhood dreams were gone. First, my roly-polies caused me a painful skin disease healed by a veterinarian who was a friend of my father. Then, my parents began a long, painful, and arduous divorce process, which lasted many years. Physical and verbal abuse grew in my home on almost a daily basis. The Divine Intimacy and oneness I once knew had vanished. Now, a brutal sense of survival was the order of the day, inside our own home and outside in the violent city streets of Sao Paulo, Brazil where I was born and raised. "I had to fight back. I had to learn to defend myself - and my little sister, to the extent possible - if I was going to have a chance in life," I thought. And, so I did! I fought back. I fought my brother, father, boyfriends, mother, culture, government, neighbors, whoever was threatening was to be resisted fiercely. Unbeknownst to me, I was living a state of defensiveness and againstness that seemed appropriate and necessary at the time. I embodied the defense strategies I felt would protect me without recognizing that they were also alienating me from the love, oneness, and intimacy I once knew.

My desperate efforts to rescue the old, familiar sense of oneness and Divine Intimacy were fruitless because I was seeking in all the wrong places: love relationships, career, achievements, friends, family, appearance, government, culture. I was seeking for it everywhere except inside of me. So I entered a career in law, thinking it would protect and defend myself and others and allow me to relive the harmony and fulfillment of the Divine Intimacy I knew as a child. But unfortunately, although I consider my legal career very successful, it failed to bring me back to the Divine Intimacy I once knew.

I looked for intimacy in my love relationships. But, although I loved deeply, none of my love partners could deliver over time the same sense of Divine Intimacy I lived in childhood.

I became a mother and gave birth to two incredible children who fill me with joy, inspiration, and enthusiasm. Yet, they, too, can't offer me that same sense of Divine Intimacy I remember as a child. With all the joys and rewards of motherhood, it can be easy to find myself over-responsible for my children's choices and fail to allow myself the same state of being I once held as a child.

My search for Divine intimacy has taken me far and abroad. It gave me the courage to emigrate from my native country, the strength to partake in an intense 15-year career as a lawyer, and the dedication to motherhood. I failed many relationships, divorced once, married twice, and learned from each one of them. I birthed two amazing children and suffered from a chronic physical illness before I came to the realization that the Divine Intimacy I was looking for had been waiting right in the depths of my own being all along. Upon that realization, I began my sacred healing journey through self-observation, self-awareness, meditation, mediation, reflection, contemplation, curiosity, spirituality, psychology, philosophy, and other traditions.

Interestingly, it took me at least a decade before I could remember my childhood experience of Divine Intimacy, which fulfilled me with an overwhelming sense of absolute oneness with existence. This state had been completed erased from my memories and only revealed itself again after a decade of dedicated inner work. As far as the trauma was concerned, it took even longer, another 5 five years or so. Only very recently have I recognized the extent of the trauma and abuse I went through in adolescence. I carried the abuse as a 'normal' part of the culture for a long while. Through continuous inner work, I have developed to examine the trauma I suffered from a place of compassion and elevation. I have learned to accept the pain underneath the trauma in loving ways. I have dedicated myself to the awakening of many dormant and unconscious parts of me and my heritage, which remain unconscious. What I know now is that the inner work of awakening is infinite. It continues unfolding in unexpected ways. It is unique to each person. It is sacred in the ways it obeys specific universal laws. My prayer and intention are to continue sharpening my ability to comprehend, understand, receive, and share my life experiences as blessings serving the unfoldment of Spirit* on earth for the highest good of all.

This book is a collection of meditations depicting the most transformational portions of my healing journey towards Divine Intimacy up until now. It marks the starting point of a way of living that focuses on intimately knowing myself by entering into deeper levels of connection with many aspects within me. It has been a constant exchange of revealing myself and receiving revelations from the universe.

This book is a love story filled with tears, misinterpretations, drama, joys, revelations, successes. This book is the story of my ego separating from God's infinite love and finally taking steps to return to unity in God again. This book is the story of my ego falling madly in love with my soul. This book is the story of my ego rediscovering the greatest love there is - God's love - through Divine Intimacy and declaring its dependency upon It.

I call myself forward into my Spiritual Heart* and humbly ask Spirit for guidance in expressing myself fully and authentically. I ask God to awaken me more deeply into oneness with the Divine* and use me for the highest service and the highest good of all. I ask the Christ Consciousness to deliver grace and ease in this journey of following His footsteps humbly, lovingly, and joyfully serving myself and others. Finally, I ask God to protect, surround and enlighten every one of us in each step of our way. I sincerely hope this book is used in service and inspiration to others who may be seeking a similar endeavor.

ACKNOWLEDGEMENTS

I am deeply grateful to everyone who has supported me throughout my journey to Divine Intimacy, particularly my teachers: John-Roger (J-R)*, John Morton*, Deborah Martinez*; my reader, Robbie Burt*; and all the staff, volunteers, assistants, readers and students of the Doctorate of Spiritual Sciences (DSS)*, offered by the Peace Theological Seminary and College of Philosophy (PTS)*, during which I have written much of the contents of this book.

I am also profoundly thankful to my teachers Drs. Ron and Mary Hulnick*; and all the staff, readers, and volunteers committed to the mission of communicating the principles and practices of Spiritual Psychology worldwide at the University of Santa Monica*.

I honor with special appreciation my doctor, Philipp Barr, who has guided me towards healing in all levels: physical, emotional, mental, and spiritual, and showed me the path for transformation.

I am incredibly thankful to my beloved husband, Mike, for his love and strength and our children, Katlyn and Koady, for their unconditional love for me. I am grateful also for my brother-in-law, Laurence Lyons Murphy, for his amazing teachings, and my dear friends Nancy Esguerra,

Jackie Peterson, Paula Majeski, Jennie Linthorst, and Helen Bradley for their heartfelt support and inspiration.

My deepest gratitude goes to my dear family: my dad, Adilson; my mom, Neusa; my sister, Idarly; my brother, Ilton; my aunt, Norma; and my extended family and friends for sharing with me the experiences and dimensions upon which I can come to know myself.

1. A HIGHER PLAN

WHERE I AM FROM

I am from a far away land where
things were never quiet, calm.
I am from a busy, overpopulated city
with cars honking on the streets,
traffic lights, people everywhere.

I am from a house of terrors where my brother's bullying
kept me and my sister locked in a room every afternoon.

I am from a little messy bedroom decorated
with cherry tree wooden furniture,
where my sister and I spent our afternoons,
living as prisoners of a culture of machismo;
in which my father didn't care, my
mom was too tired to care.

Beating was normal.
Nothing that really needed attention.
A reason to laugh on the silly kids.

It was years of silent abuse, silent
violence, silent survival
inside the house of terrors.

I am from a garden of cactuses
with trees filled by long, hard, pointy leaves.
There, I met my friends: the rolly-pollies.
There, I played with my dog.
There, I ran wild in my imagination.
There, I was happy.
Until I became sick from the roly-polies;
my dog gave her last breath in my arms.
In that same cactus garden,
I cried all the tears of my stolen innocence.
The house was invaded by robbers
with loaded guns pointed to my sister's head.
We left our house with fear and tears
to a little sad apartment
a few blocks away, very near.

I am from a pink tiled backyard with
vases of ferns and flowers
which I planted with my loving heart and hands.

I am from hot tropical humid summer afternoons
when my dad would climb with us to the roof
to have us bathe in the gray, cement
water tank of our five-star "resort".

*I am from a bright yellow room holding
pictures of dogs, puppies
as well as my dream to be a vet or an astronaut one day.*

*I am from my mom's clothing store, where I dressed
in all different sizes, ages, styles,
trying hard to find the perfect mask
to hide my imperfections.*

*I am from vacations at my grandfather's beach house
where the sun was too hot to breath;
the family of uncles, aunts, cousins,
everyone gathered together in little spaces,
sharing meals, laughters, gossip, arguments
while playing card games through the night.*

*I am from a dirty old public school, also
from a traditional Catholic prep school.*

*I am from an authoritative, "my way
or the highway" loving mom,
also, from a progressive, liberal, out-
of-the box kind of dad.*

*I am from samba dancing all night long parties
also, from strict classic ballet techniques.*

I am from the violent, over-crowded city of Sao Paulo,
also, from the paradisiac beaches,
islands, forests of Brazil.

I am from the land of those who "have nothing"
also, those who "have way too much."

I am from a land of disparities, injustices, paradoxes
where very little made any sense at all to me.

I am from the land of opposite extremes
struggling to find a middle that never seemed to appear.

I am from a place I barely remember.
I am from a resistance to even go back there.
I am from a hurt deep inside of a place
that I haven't made peace with.
I am from a place I don't understand
and don't wish to come back to.

WHEN GOD IS PRESENT

When God speaks, there is peace.
When God speaks, there is clear sense of direction.
When God shows, there is revelation in the inner eyes.
When it's God's time, there is flow, synchronicity.
When God is present, there is nothing else.

DIVINE PRESENCE

I feel the presence of the Holy Spirit as all accepting.
My emotions, feelings, thoughts,
desires lose their grip on me.
I am amidst a white misty fog of quiet exhilaration,
which moves me softly as if I am a cloud in Heaven.

GOD IN ME

I have always wondered
how come the God of the Old testament
is judgmental, punishing
with floods, wars, destruction, killing the wicked;
while the God of the New Testament is loving,
patient, unconditionally filled with grace?
Why would God change?
Did God evolve or change His mind?
A supreme God wouldn't have to change.

It has finally dawned on me:
the Bible is a mirror of my consciousness.
I was born as one in God.
At some point, I was introduced to
judgments, punishments.
I started to feel separated, thrown
out of the Garden of Eden.

I became possessive, jealous, territorial.
I grew with commandments of right and wrong,
beautiful and ugly, good and bad.
I entered the inevitable consciousness of duality,
which every human being eventually embraces.
I became the dominant God of the Old Testament.
I destroyed myself emotionally numerous
times with broken hearts,
betrayed friendships, looking for my
identity out in the world.
After fears and pains, I finally learned
an easier path: the way of Christ.
The path of love, grace, forgiveness.
I became the New Testament.

Now I know why God changes throughout the Bible.
Because the Bible tells the story of the God within me.
After all, God is in me, as I am in God.

THE EDGE OF MY ABYSS

I am connected to a higher plane, to
the sustainer, the Holy Spirit,
that which gives my suffering a meaning,
keeps me walking upwards,
makes me look for the blessings,
saves me from the edge of my abyss.

GOODNESS

Everyone suffers, complains, despairs
about that which they don't like or don't agree
or wished it was different in this world.
Listen here everyone:
when God created the world,
he said" It's very GOOD".
He did not say it's fun, fair, beautiful,
perfect, "as you wish", or any of that.
He said, clearly and loudly: "It's very good"
Why did He say so?
Because goodness is the intention in all creation.
Whether you like it or not, agree with
it or not, wish it or not...
Who cares?
None of that matters, not even a bit.
With all due respect to your sense of self-importance,
God couldn't care less about your opinion.
It is your job to care about God's "opinion";
and he has only one opinion: "It's Good".
Now, it is your responsibility to find the
goodness in everything, in everyone;
whatever, whoever is in front of you,
find the goodness;
do not waste any opportunity to find the goodness.
Don't go around it, turn your back
to it, pretend it is not there;

or even worse, keep looking back,
or imagining it forward.
Just go through it,
in the moment, right here, right now.
Look, search, seek until you find goodness
as it was originally intended.
Why?
Because finding goodness is finding God.

TRUST

I trust this universe as the mirror of my personality.
I trust this universe as a reflection of me, in
its beauty as well as in its calamities.
I trust this universe to be magical, mystical,
because it manifests a customized
version of what I attract or need
for my highest learning, my highest good.
Whether I like or dislike it is completely irrelevant.
There is an energetic story hidden in my spiritual DNA*
unfolding itself beyond my comprehension.
The ultimate goal is to return to the
highest vibration of God.

2. RECEPTIVITY

OPEN TO RECEIVE

What does it mean to be open to receive?
It is certainly not the sense of
entitlement my ego knows well.
It is the gracious gratitude of a warm embrace
by the comforting morning sun.
It is the gentle look of a cute puppy when
caressed by my loving hand.
It is the serenity of a healthy baby
feeding from his mother's breasts.
It is the sweet aroma of a rose which
petals are starting to open.
It is the exquisite beauty of a little bird
singing on my window sill.

RECEIVE

Receiving is the foundation of life.
By receiving life, I am born.
By receiving the breath, I am alive.
By receiving the sun, the rain, I am sustained.

By receiving others, I know myself
By receiving, I am!

CHANGE

When change knocks on the door,
do I open, consider what it is offering me?
Do I hide behind the door, pretend no one is home?
Do I send it away, reject it like it's the wrong address?
Do I doubt, investigate, check it out?
Yes, all of the above, I have done them all.
Which one will I do this time?
Doubt, investigate, check it out, first.
Then, open, consider the offer.
Lean into it, see what it has in storage for me.

INSIDE AND OUT

Receiving inside is so different than
receiving on the outside.
On the inside, my receiving is bounty, abundant, infinite,
the outside doesn't do it justice.

DIVINE INTIMACY

Divine Intimacy is a place where I open
myself to receive abundantly.
No guilt, no thinking I should do
more, give more, be more.
Divine Intimacy receives fully, graciously, gracefully,
in the spirit that is given by the Lord to his children.

JOGGING

I was jogging on the beach when, all of the sudden,
the keys for the chain in my bike fell into the sand.
I kneeled down trying to find them without success.
I caressed the sand all around.
Nothing.
I asked myself: why?
What is the symbolism of this strange occurrence?
Losing my keys?
Caressing the sand?
What was the blessing of this occurrence?
I sat on the sand for some reflection time
when right in front of my very eyes, very near the shore,
I saw five dolphins and a seagull
dancing happily in the ocean water.
What a gift!
A private show!

A holy moment,
which I would have missed if I had not lost my keys.

DISCIPLINE

It takes a lifetime to learn to love life
when it doesn't behave the way I want.

---

3. INTENTIONS

MY INTENTION

My intention is not to resist, but to allow,
not the pulls of the world, but the action of Spirit.
It is a subtle dance, with delicate and intricate moves.
I am practicing this new dance
knowing there will be mistakes.
And, that's ok!

MY AFFIRMATIONS

I am enjoying radiance through vibrant
health; elegant beauty; and

*the exhilarating relaxation of being
free from disturbances.*

*I am in a state of bliss, as I enthusiastically
engage with life, and spontaneously partake
of the joy and amusement of being alive.*

*I am lovingly observing what is;
while recognizing and enjoying goodness,
beauty, and blessings; and
knowingly using my gifts and talents to
love and serve those around me.*

*I am in a transcendental state of supreme contentment,
aware that I am in the center of my Soul,
trusting and rejoicing on Earth as in Spirit.*

*I am setting clear simple intentions
as often as I remember.*

*I am upgrading my opinions, wishes, lusts,
desires, limitations, illusions, etc.
to God.*

I am allowing the Compassionate Spirit* to fill me.

I am neutrally observing reality for what it is.

I am giving myself into S.Es*.

*I am accepting myself and others in
every and all expressions.*

*I am in a state of bliss, humor and amusement as
I recognize, appreciate and express
the funny side of life.*

*I am in the flow of God's energy as It works through me
with grace, ease and enthusiasm.*

---

4. ACCEPTANCE

SPRING IS BACK

*Spring is back blooming newly born flowers in my heart.
Bright colors are popping out under the warm sunshine.
It's time to travel to that joy that hibernated quietly inside
during the cold months of winter.*

SELF-ACCEPTANCE

What is self-acceptance?
Is it to accept my greed, my limitations,
the dark parts of me?
Is it to claim my beauty, my wisdom, my femininity?
Is it to be ok with eating a pot of ice cream
with a bag of chocolate cookies?
What is to accept myself?
I've experienced all of the above.
I've learned they are traps of desire, sensation,
lust doomed for endless dissatisfaction.
The more I get, the more I want.
That's the trap of "pleasing" myself.
Self-acceptance is not self-pleasing.
Stop it!
"Fast, pray, know God" I hear in my head.
"Ooops, is self-acceptance self-deprivation?"
I go from one extreme to another:
from fasting to indulging,
from celibacy to promiscuity,
Is self-acceptance a matter of moderation?
What is moderation anyway?
A never ending pursuit of seeking a middle
by constantly falling outside of it?
I feel like I need to join an AA meeting
"My name is Inely. I am a human. I am addicted to life.

To something in life that feels good,
tastes good, looks good.
I am addicted. I never cease to
want to satisfy my senses."

THE COLORS OF LOVE

Love has many colors.
In fact, love has all colors.
There is not one color that is not loving.
The more you express your loving
in a wider variety of colors,
the more you allow who you are to manifest in the Light.
Loving is the acceptance of this fact.
Accepting all colors of love as beautiful.
They all play a part in the variety of
the rainbow of your heart.
Expansion is happening to you right now.
Your heart is expanding into colors that
you would have judged in the past.
No judgement necessary anymore.
Accept.
All your colors are radiant, beautiful, perfect.
You are made in the image of the Creator,
so what is there to judge?

MONSTERS IN THE CLOSET

What monsters have you been
keeping inside your closet?
What fears have been keeping you awake at night?
What are the horrid things you are
afraid even to think about?
Yes, the monsters in your closet, what are they?
I thought I had grown out of the childish
stories of monsters in the closet,
but the monster stories still persist in my consciousness.
I have now achieved greater sophistication
around the horror stories I tell myself.
The pattern, however, is still the same, still intact.
I still painfully believe the monsters in my closet are real.
I live with them.
I make decisions based on them.
How many times I've completed the sentence
"what if...." in my head ending with an
awful disastrous story which leads me into
turning one corner instead of another?
I suddenly woke up to the illusory nature of
my fears, the monsters in my closet.
Today, I painted my monster.
I looked at his dark vicious eyes.
I talked to him.
This is what he told me:

*"I am the one who is killing you, who
is sabotaging, draining you.
I am living off your blood. I drink
of your blood every day.
I satisfy my thirst by drinking of your blood.
I am the vampire inside of you.
The one who wants to kill you and all the
stupid goodness you pretend to put out there.
I am the devil who lives inside of you.
I am here to scare you away, to put you in your place, to
make you bleed to death until you shut up, cry, go away.
I am here to stop you, put an end to you.
If you believe in me, you are dead.
I guard the gate to the next frontier;
the transcendence of your own made up material;
the surpassing of everything you bought into.
I am reflecting back to you the monsters you've created.
Now, deal with me.
Unless, of course, you un-create me."
In this dreadful dialogue, I realized his voice is my voice.
I am the one scaring myself.
I am the one with the monsters.
I am living with the monsters I create.
So, I broke free.
I started laughing at myself, at my own fears,
at the monsters I put in my closet.
There is simply nothing to be afraid of.
There is only life.*

There is only love.
There is only what is right here, right now.
Everything else are the monsters I put in my closet.

JUDGMENT

I feel liberated, free in my expressions,
the ones I enjoy, such as poetry;
the ones I do not enjoy, such as anger.
For the freer I am in my highs, the freer I am in my lows.
Expression comes within a spectrum.
How could I judge my expression
when I am only the vessel?
If I am not to judge my own
expressions; either high or low,
then how could I even think of judging
the expression of others?

---

5. COMPASSION

MAKING FRIENDS

I am today,
with my rights and wrongs;
my good's and bad's,

with all of me.
We are friends again.

AM I REALLY WHAT THEY SAY?

What would have been of us if, at
the moment of crucifixion,
Christ doubted himself?
What if he had wondered if he was really a criminal?
After all, he was being crucified as one,
in between two other criminals.

Doubt did not enter His consciousness
because he was filled with compassionate forgiveness:
"Forgive them, Father, for they know not
what they do," is what He said.

Then, why is it that I doubt myself based on
what other people say or think of me?
Why do I even wonder: am I really what they say?

IS THIS WHAT I HAVE CALLED LOVE?

I observed myself today loving the
outside, the shell, the superfluous,
judging the target of my loving as

beautiful or ugly; caring or selfish;
should this or should that...

I observed love as a fragile connection
with a fragile target:
a connection in constant change.

This connection I have called love
changes with every judgment;
is inflicted with pain, also pleasure
that's never sustainably fulfilling,
because it soon changes again.

Love has been a fragile connection to a fragile target.

That's been how I've loved everyone:
my mom, my kids, my partner, my friends,
my family, my pets, myself.

My fragile connections are heavy with expectations:
It has to be loyal.
It has to be lasting.
It has to be fun, honest, pure, innocent,
spiritual, wise, handsome, polite,
so much more.

In the end of every day
I judge my disguised love against all my expectations.

Is it fulfilling?
Is it right, good, fun for me?
The answers are never the same.
They too change daily, often, many
times over during the day.

I observe myself in this fragile love again and again.
I now laugh loudly.
Really?
Is this what I've called love?

DISCOVERY OF THE OBVIOUS

I have made the greatest discovery of the century:
I live holographically in many dimensions at once.
All my inner voices, my different masks
can not fit a linear perspective.
It would be like watching a 3D movie
without the proper lenses.
The image would be fussy, unclear, confusing,
conducive to judgment, criticism. My self-judgment
has been a by-product of my ignorance
of my multidimensional nature.
I have a physical body, yet I am not my body.
I have an emotional body, yet I am not my emotions.
I have a mental body, filled with
comparisons, analysis, judgments,

but, thank goodness, I am not them either.
Who am I then?
I am the one who is lovingly growing
in awareness of all of me.
What a huge, holy discovery of the obvious that is!

MANY BODIES

My consciousness has many bodies:
physical, astral, emotional, mental, unconscious, soul,
except for the soul, which is unchangeable,
all of them are dualistic, unstable.
In the soul, I find consistency, sustainability, oneness.
Let my soul guide all my other bodies.

How do I distinguish the voice of my soul
from the voices of my dualistic bodies?
The soul has peace, knowing, clarity, direction.
My dualistic bodies, anxiety,
uncertainty, doubt, confusion.

BODY OUTFIT

To be born in a human body is to wear a sensorial outfit
which experiences itself by touching,
smelling, tasting, seeing, hearing.

My sensorial experiences are translated by my mind into
good vs. bad,
innocent vs. guilty,
right vs. wrong,
moral vs. immoral.

My sensorial experiences are
translated by my emotions into
worthy vs. unworthy,
pleasant vs. unpleasant,
pure vs. shameful.

In the end, I forget I am not the translation.
I am not the sensorial outfit.
I am not the thoughts of my mind.
I am not the emotions.

I am the one inside who wears the outfit,
guides the experiences,
observes the thoughts, emotions,
becomes aware of the no-thing-ness I am.

6. SACRIFICE

TITHING

Sacrifice is the tithing* of my attachments.

THE STORM

*The shadows of darkness approach
me slowly with words of distrust,
feelings of frustrated resentment, sarcasm, resistance.
It's a storm with clouds denser and denser,
winds that blow pitilessly,
air that gets heavier with each breath.
I sacrifice it all, the dark clouds, the
strong winds, the heavy air.
I sacrifice my thoughts, my should's,
my would's, my need to be right.
I enter the sunshine of Spirit,
bathe in the sweet balm of joy,
smell the delicious aroma of love.
The storm is gone.*

I ALWAYS THOUGHT

I always thought sacrifice was difficult, painful, useless.
I always thought a life of sacrifice would be a waste.
I always thought sacrifice was about
suppressing, resisting.
Little did I know...
sacrifice is salvation, life, renewal,
detachment, openness, receiving,
resurrection, rebirth, restart.
Sacrifice is what life is all about.

LUST

Lust is wonderful, but Love is infinitely better.

THE CONSCIOUSNESS OF HOLDING

I have compassion for myself, my
journey, where it's taken me.
I see amazing aspects of me.
I see not-so-amazing aspects of me.
I have been holding positions against
the not-so-amazing parts of me.
I have also been holding onto the amazing parts of me.
In both cases, I am in the consciousness of holding.

In that consciousness, I will never win.
Holding onto the awesomeness is the same
as holding against the ugliness.
It's the same consciousness of holding after all.

How do I get out of the consciousness of holding?
Who am I without my consciousness of holding?
Is it possible to live without a consciousness of holding?

The answer to all those questions is "I don't know".
But I must try, I must start with what I have, where I am.
I must start by sacrificing my attachments to
good and bad; beautiful and ugly; right and wrong.

Yes, it sounds like auto-flagellation.
Yes, it feels like auto-flagellation.

It sounds negative.
It feels negative.
It overrides a huge part of me.

However, I don't know what else to do.

Moderation is the word that comes to mind.
I can approach sacrifice with moderation.
Yes. Moderation is my way of approaching sacrifice.
Little by little.
Dimming up the light.

A NEW FRIEND

I have a new friend.
Her name is Sacrifice.
I met her abandoned on a dark corner.
She was surprised when I approached her.
No one has cared for her.
She looked like a ghost, a demon.
She has never been heard, understood.
She has never been looked at in the eye.
Until this blessed day, when I approached her.
Out of my own despair, there was no
one else to hold me, but her.
So, I walked slowly towards that little fragile
figure sitting alone in the shadow.
I stepped slowly towards her in hesitancy.
She kept looking down, as if she
hadn't notice my presence.
She has been ignored, mocked, spitted on.
I persisted on moving carefully towards her.
I wasn't really sure either about her.
She was dressed in dirty, rotten
rags, but it didn't stop me.
I really had no other choice.
She was the only one around.
I gave one more step forward, called her name.
She raised her face, looked at me
straight, deep into my eyes.

To my shock, I saw the most sublime view
my eyes could have ever seen.
A child, a young child, with eyes filled with
love, hope, enthusiasm, excitement.
Her face sparkled like the brightest star in the sky.
Her lips, pink as rose, opened themselves
revealing the most angelic smile.
She sat up taller, reached towards me.
Without further thought, I reached back,
held her soft little sweet hands.
We hugged like old friends.
We have been playing together now day after day.
She wipes away my tears, fears, doubts, judgments.
She holds my imperfections, my
humanness, my darkness.
She shows me the horizon ahead, the
sun coming behind the mountains,
the waterfall in the forest, the flowers, the birds.
She smells like a baby, giggles like a toddler,
plays like a child, discovers like a teenager,
loves like a young adult, serves like a mother,
intuits like a wise elder.
I am still not really sure about her.
Who is she? How does she do it?
Where does she come from?
But I don't I care.
The more I ask, the less I know.
The more I experience her, the more I am.

MY BELOVEDS

Sacrifice is now my friend.
I hold it in my right hand.
In the left, I hold hands with forgiveness.
We, the three of us, walk happily, skipping, singing
innocent melodies in joyful rhymes
for I am no longer alone.
My beloveds are right here.

SWEET BALM OF JOY

Sacrifice, my sweet balm of joy.
It takes away my sorrows,
It washes away my terror, my fears, my pain.
In a moment of divine connection,
it wraps me in the arms of the beloved
as a precious gift of love.
I am healed, fulfilled, surrounded
by this experiential knowing
that I am not my body, my thoughts,
neither my emotions.
I am the beloved who holds me dearly
in universal sustenance,
in communion with the ultimate power of the Creator.

7. GRATITUDE

GRATITUDE

The difference between taking and receiving is gratitude.

THANKSGIVING

In this day of thanksgiving, my
heart is filled with gratitude
for all that is around me:
all that works in my life, all that doesn't work in my life;
all that went as I had planned, all
that went completely wrong.

I discover that gratitude has no relationship with results.
Results may prompt gratitude or it may not.
Gratitude lives independently of
my successes or failures.
Gratitude is a sense of connection
with the greater universe.

Gratitude is a magical way of being part
of the perfect order of everything,

despite of the fact that it all seems
so completely imperfect.

THE TRAVELER*

It is filled with gratitude that I end this day.
The Traveler supports me, holds me
in the most loving ways.
The Traveler hovers around me, catches me when I fall.
The Traveler embraces me, accepts me completely.
I am loved, adored.
I am.

---

8. BREATHING

MY BREATH

My breath is the most profound discovery
of the obvious I have ever had,
so close yet invisible;
so infinite yet simple;
so majestic yet ordinary.
I love my breath as a baby's first
sight of his mother's eyes.

THE ARMS OF THE UNIVERSE

My breath is the comforting arms of the Universe
embracing me warmly in every sacred moment.

MY BREATH AND ME

I found my breath to be
my loyal companion,
my comfort zone,
my security blanket.
It's a presence of abundance constantly supporting me.
In my breath, I am completely fulfilled.
In my breath, I am provided for.
In my breath, I am one with all.
In my breath, I am loved.
In my breath, I am Spirit, Spirit is me.
In my breath, I am!
Only me and my breath, what else do I need?

I LOVE MY BREATH

I love my breath.
It inspires me
to be bolder,
to be bigger,

to be higher,
to be taller,
to be more beautiful,
to be more than I ever thought I could be.
My breath is wise, creative,
the breeze of the universe renewing me in every moment
like a refreshing bath from the fountain of life
washing clean every atom, each cell with gratitude.

MY BEST FRIEND

My breath is my best friend.
My breath is my miracle.
My miracle of creation happening at
every second right inside of me.
All animals, all plants breath.
Breathing is part of life everywhere,
yet, my breath is special.
My breath makes me special,
because I am awaken to it,
because I have come to realize the glory of it.
In its glory, I too am glorified with the
experience of infinite love
I am!

HUG

One day, I was so deeply grateful for my breath
I wished I could hug it.
Then, I realized
I was already being hugged by it.

MY BREATH IS

My breath knows no judgment or comparisons.
My breath knows no duality, doubts or fears.
My breath knows no-thing.
My breath simply breathes.
My breath simply is.

TODAY

Today, I heard my breath saying
how beautiful I am,
how loved I am,
how precious I am.
Today, I let my breath show me
God hugging me,
God loving me,
God right here with me
unconditionally,

constantly,
tirelessly,
in every breath.

THE TRUTH

When my mind is confused, my breath is still.
When my body is busy, my breath is calm.
When my emotions are in turmoil, my breath is stable.
My breath is the opposite of me,
remembering me to the truth of who I really am.

MY PEACE

My breath is my peace;
my everything I need
in every moment.

MORE TO SAY

I could write all day my love for my breath.
I could sing all my life my gratitude for my breath.
Yet, there would be more to write, say, sing.

9. SPIRITUAL EXERCISES*

RECIPE FOR ENLIGHTENMENT

Surrendering my goals, desires,
expectations to that which is.
Is that the recipe to fulfillment?

Quieting my mind, chanting the names
of the Lord in active meditation,
letting go of the busyness that disturbs my inner peace.
Is that the recipe of enlightenment?

How is one to know what works or
doesn't work if not by trying?
How is one to know how to live love if not by doing?
How is one to know how to find
oneself if not by getting lost?

I WISH

I wish I could sit here to write away all
the voices I hear in my head.
Some voices are yelling loud to be heard.

Some are whispering quiet hoping
no one will hear them.

I wish I could sit here to reveal
myself entirely, completely,
turning all the cards,
grieving all my pains,
expressing all my joys.

I wish I could just sit here
me, myself and I
in perfect peace with each other.

WHAT A STRANGE FEELING

It is quiet, dark, late.
I am peacefully waiting to hear voices
ready to be expressed.
Nothing comes forward.
Inside me, all is quiet too.
What a strange feeling.
I am not used to such peace
Is it boring?
Is it exciting?
Is it awkward?
All of the above.
The question is what lies underneath this quietude?

The universal sound.
The golden thread to God.
Where are you, God?
In the infinite of this quietude.
How do I find you?
Lifting out of my mind.
I sense immensity, an antigravity floating
sensation of weightless matter.

I HEAR GOD SPEAK

Sacrifice and silence pave the channel
through which I receive the word of God.
Inner reflection is my dialogue with the divine.
Nature is divine music which creates
ambiance, inspiration.
Physical exercise, breathing, sweating is
the pumping of my inner machine,
preparing to receive the word of God.
I hear God speak…

10. WRITING

WRITING

*Sometimes I wish to write not because
I have something to say,
but because there is something
waiting to be said by me,
which I have no idea what it is.
It feels a lot like vomiting the excess
noise of my own mind,
so I may get a glimpse of quiet
connection with who I truly am.*

FROZEN MOMENTS ON A PAPER

*When I saw people older than me,
I used to think they knew what they were doing.
They knew who they were.
They knew how to be their age.
As I age myself, I realize I have no
clue how to be my age.
I suspect no one has any clue either.
We are all doing our age for the very first
time without much instruction.*

Then, comes poetry,
frozen moments on a piece of paper.
It's a glimpse of what others have done, felt, thought.
I hear their cries, their joys.
I identify.
I no longer feel alone doing life for the first time.
Someone else has done it before me.
They shared it in writing.
In their sharing, we connect, we become one.
They bring sense to my non-sense.
They bring communion to my solitude.
They give me an instruction manual for my life.

TO BE A POET

To be a poet is to suffer happily;
to enjoy suffering like a delicious meal:
smell it, chew it slowly, examine it, watch it, touch it,
then put it down in words.

To be a poet is to go deep down into my suffering,
so as to break it in letters and words,
which others will read
to feel their own suffering anew.

To be a poet is to open one's heart,
share one's joy, dissect one's suffering;
then put them all for inspection, retrospection, extraction.

ART

Art allows softness in difficult conversations,
explains things, makes connections
without the rigidity of my mind.
Art distracts my mind,
so that my understanding may happen through my soul.
Art says what my mind doesn't know.

LITTLE VOICE

There is this little voice inside who
thinks my writing is stupid.
She laughs arrogantly on the face of my simplicity.
Little she knows, however, how much fun I have.
For I have nothing to prove, no one to please.
Only a huge heart waiting to be shared!

SHE DID IT FOR LOVE

There is a part inside who urges to tell her story.
She needs to make sure others know her actions
have all been done in the name of love.
She did not please everyone.
In fact, she betrayed those she cared deeply.
She did not follow the rules, traditions, expectations.
In fact, she violated them.
She was not the role model others may have wished.
In fact, she was human, fallible.
She wasn't understood by her own tribe.
In fact, she was judged, cursed, crucified by them.
Yet, no matter whether she was right or wrong,
or her actions were good or bad.
All she did, she did it for Love!

I WANT TO KNOW

I want to know what love really is.
Is it the pursuit of my passions, pleasures?
The excitement of knowing the
fulfillment of this very moment?
I want to know who speaks in my heart.
Is it the voice of my desires?
Or, the voice of my knowing?
My lightness or my darkness?

I want to know where does my passion come from?
Is it motivation to fulfill my life's purpose?
Is it attachment to earthly goals which
will eventually vanish in pain?
I want to know how can I trust my heart if
I can't even figure out who is speaking in there?
I want to know how can I follow my
dreams and yet be detached?
How I can love intensely and yet let it go?
How I can be in this world without being of this world?
How can I live this insane paradox called life?
How can one be "conscious" in the crossroad of life?
I want to know what really matters in this non-sense?

OUTSIDE SEARCH

I've searched for myself in things outside of me.
I've searched for my phenomenal me
in the shape of my body,
the youth of my skin,
the flexibility of my muscles.

I've searched for my joy in a romantic soulful partner,
in the blue Caribbean beach of a five star resort,
in the luxury of a lifestyle surrounded by ease, grace.
I've searched outside of me for that
which I believed would bring me

the joy of my phenomenal me.
But, is my phenomenal me the effect
of joy, or the cause of it?

INSIDE THE CAVE

Inside the cave of my own being I
scream and yell, but no one hears.
I sing, celebrate but no one joins me.
I die, resurrect a thousand times but no one knows.
Inside the cave of my own being, there
is a whole entire universe—
unknown, undiscovered, unrevealed.
Inside the cave of my own being, there
is a bomb waiting to explode.
There is a fountain waiting impatiently for
the opportunity to water the world!

INNER FILES

There is a list of undesired material
saved in my inner files.
I rarely look at them, never really share them.
They have been stored as trash.
Sadly, however, never fully discarded.

HIDING OUT

I hide behind a world of appearances.
It is not bad enough to change.
It is not good enough to thrive.

I protect my weakness with a busy to do list,
filled with endless useless items,
to cover up my heart's true purpose.

I hide behind my friends with nice loving conversations.
I hide behind my children
with their homework, dinnertime, after school activities.

I even hide behind myself:
my books, clients, dance classes,
my pictures, stories, my facebook page.

Then, I wonder:
who wakes me up at night?
What is my meaningful contribution?
What is my soul's purpose?

It is to be true;
to reveal the truth within my heart;
to come out of hiding.
to be mySelf!

Then comes my mind with critics, doubts:
"you have too much free time to think";
"unhappiness is having the luxury of time to
think about what makes you unhappy."
So, back to ground zero
I don't know anymore
who talks in my head.

EMOTIONS

Moments of emotions
when tears fall from my heart
but no-one can see them.

Tears of gratitude for achievements fulfilled.
Tears of what could have been but never was,
for dreams never achieved, left undone.

Tears of satisfaction, also separation.
Tears of pride, also regret.

They all mash up as the bundle of my life,
hidden in the quietude of my heart.
Once in awhile, they shed a silent tear
which no one sees.

WHO IS IT?

Who is it that yells at me to be perfect
so that I can be happy?
Who is it that tells me to be strong, independent,
so that I will not need anyone else to take care of me?
Who forces me to be smart, talented,
pretty, unique, and much more
so that I can prove my worth?
Who wakes me up at night to say that
if I am not the perfect mom,
my kids will be screwed up?
Who gives me ideals of eternal youth,
beauty for me to achieve?
Whose voices scream in my ears
in the silence of the night?
Voices of shame, guilt, unworthiness, who are you?
You hide, masquerade, then, all of the sudden,
jump out of the closet when I least expect.
I don't believe you anymore, but you still scare me.
I know you are not even real, an illusion of
my mind, yet you are still ugly to see.
I know you are powerless, yet my mind
keeps feeding you into survival.
I know you come from someone somewhere
doing the very best they could.
I know you come from someone's best
attempt to live their definition of "love."

I know you no longer serve me.
I know you.
Now, could you just move
from shame into freedom,
from unworthy into divinity?
Could you just be one who does no wrong,
who is inherently beautiful,
who is a light shining bright,
laughing for no special reason?

THE 'BECAUSE' OF MY UPSETS

The same consciousness that focuses
on the "because'" of my upsets
also focuses on the "because" of my joys.
This is the consciousness of victimization which
seeks outside of me the reasons for
what is happening within me,
be it upsetting or joyful.
It has been my loyal friend, my savior, my salvation
ever since I was first born.
It has cried when I was hungry, hurt or wet.
It has smiled when I was warm, content, full.
It has signaled my reactions to the outside world.
Initially, as a baby, for purposes of survival.
Later, as I grew up, for comfort or preference.
I still cry when I am hurt.

I still smile when I am content.
I still use my reactions to manipulate the outer world
so I can get which I believe to be
the source of my fulfillment.
I still wait for the source of my comfort, my joy
to come to me as the charming
prince who will save my day.
Just like the baby who cried for survival,
I am now the victim who expects salvation.
I am the prisoner of a deep-seated misbelief that
my fulfillment is to be brought to me from outside.

ADRENALINE

There is a feeling in the pit of my stomach—
tight knots of unknown, like butterflies.
I don't want to eat, sleep, relax.
I am in high alert.
It gives me chills, a strange kind of energy.

I felt it before when my parents divorced.
The fear of change.
The emptiness of my dad's closets.
The chaos of endless arguments.
The pain of a broken family.

I felt it before when my kids were sick with
high fever or beginning of pneumonia,
when my husband had heart surgery,
when my neighborhood burned in wild fire.
This primal fear of something dying while I am still alive.

I felt it too in my aunt's harsh words,
my cousin's uncontrollable rage,
their suffering, threats, yelling, screaming.

I felt this emptiness numerous times.
The same knot in the pit of my stomach, lack
of hunger or sleep, energy building up.

It's been a part of Brazilian life in the tense urban streets
with armed men ready to point their guns
at my head in public traffic lights,
with poverty, misery displayed in the
sidewalks, under bridges, everywhere ;
with overcrowded, over-noisy streets
where people walk obliviously
in the midsts of dirt, graffiti, garbage.

It's been a part of my youth which even
brought me energy, mad energy,
but energy, nonetheless, which assisted
me with things like weight loss,
or winning arguments with abusive people.

It's been a permanent part of my life which
I learned to live with, as if it is normal.

---

11. WORLD OF MIRRORS

PARENTAL HIPOCRISY

I became aware today of my parental hypocrisy.
This is when I act, think, feel exactly
the same way I tell my children not to.
It would be more authentic to say, as my father used to:
"Do as I say but don't do as I do."
I yell at my kids to tell them to stop yelling,
I get mad at them to tell them not to be so bossy;
I withhold my love from them while asking
them to act with loving kindness;
I tell them to limit their screen time while I
can't live without my lap top, cell phone.
I am a parental hypocrite.
The good thing is that I know it.

WHY?

His crankiness comes like wild fire.
It burns my joy, my desire to live, my spontaneity.

His ridiculous complaints are like storms
of pain in my sunny skies.
It feels like slow death, suffocation, asphyxiation.
Why is the universe doing this for me?
Why do I allow his superfluous
ways to suffocate my light?
Why?

OUTER REASONS

I assign an outer reason not only for
my upsets, but also for my joys.
What if I take full, and I really mean, full
responsibility for my inner landscape,
be it depressed or enthusiastic, irritated or loving,
be it whatever it may?
What if I am the only one responsible for
what is happening inside of me:
not others, not circumstances, not past life times?
If it is not the outside, then who or what
motivates my ups and downs?

PRAYER IN THE DARKNESS

My darkness is upon me.
I am tired, exhausted of being cursed,
yelled at, with meanness.
I am very sad.
I think of all I wished I had;
all that could, would, should be different.
I feel sorry for myself; a victim of my choices.
I see my reflection in a dark mirror
when I hear mean words spoken to me,
like arrows landing in my heart.
I offered myself the choice of leaving home.
The mean behavior has to leave
for my house is the Lord's house.
I must develop the responsibility for the energy I carry;
know the impact it causes on others.
I want to die, to end it all here.
Perhaps, I am dying, ending it here.
This is the hardest thing I have ever done.
I feel very alone.
I am tired of explaining things others can't hear.
I am tired of being misunderstood.
I know I can't live with myself,
with my victimization, sorrow, comparison.
I can't live with me,
yet, I can't get rid of me.
How do I throw myself out of my house?

What am I doing, Lord?
Please Compassionate Spirit come to me,
hold me in your loving arms, show me the way.

AWAKENING PAIN

Ten long years is what took me to recognize
the pattern of pain in my relationship.
It starts with an attack that sounds innocent:
"What is wrong with you?",
"I sense a heavy energy on you".
or some other sarcastic comment
meant to hurt, belittle, insult.

It is an attitude of annoyance, passive aggression,
which may seem inoffensive, yet, rides
on a wave of confrontation.

For a while, I sought within myself:
"What is wrong with me?"
I found a long list of "wrongness":
undesirable, ugly, stupid, moody, much more.

Until I realized I was none of that.
I was simply the mirror.
The mirror of someone going through the
pain of finding themselves rotten.

In that awakening, I freed myself.
I embraced the obvious fact that we
are mirrors of one another.

I realized there is no pain, only
profound misunderstandings
being reflected back and forth for
purposes of awakening.

Today, I hang onto the innocence of my loving soul
where the wrongness, the defects,
the insults, the hurt, the pain,
none of that have any meaning whatsoever.

I may seem oblivious to others, but,
inside I am awakening!!!

HAPPILY EVER AFTER

There is a deep loss living inside my being.
The loss of my "happily ever after" dream.
I experienced this loss in my first
marriage; again, in my second.

The "happily ever after" comes with
lots of trials and errors;
betrayals, lies, broken hearts.

The "happily ever after" is a hard journey
of seeing the worst of me
being shown back to me in the innocent
reflections of my beloveds,
so that I may learn to love myself anyway in all ways.

MIRROR, MIRROR ON THE WALL

I hear my daughter blaming others for her upsets?
Why does she whine and cry instead of
taking ownership, create change?
I feel victim of motherhood, of my choices,
of my perceived lack of freedom.
Mirror, mirror on the wall
who is the most victim of all?

12. MY MASKS

BLAMING BEAST

I blame my upsets on people and situations:
on my kids, my spouse, the food I eat,
the government, the poverty, the
violence, the history of humanity.

I do the same with my joys.
I blame them also on people, places, situations:
on the smile of my children's faces;
an easy, comfortable lifestyle;
the sweet smell of freshly opened roses;
the majesty of nature.

I blame the planetary alignment,
the moons, the weather,
the God of a spirituality I created
for myself to depend upon.

Whether I am upset or joyful,
to everything inside of me,
I assign a reason outside of me.

I ride in the waves of this emotional spectrum
formed by the tides of external factors
which are always outside of my control.

Whether I am high or low in my emotional spectrum,
I am still a victim of the reality I perceive around me.
I am still a prisoner of my own making.
I am still a puppet of my own illusions.

I AM AFRAID

I am afraid of voicing out the silence inside of me,
the parts of me that are kept quiet, hidden, forgotten.

I am afraid of giving importance to that which is
uncomfortable, unattended, undesirable, ugly.

I am afraid of bringing to life the
dead carnage inside of me
which I buried long ago in tears, pain, despair.

I am afraid they are bigger than
me, stronger than I think,
worse than I remember them to be.

What if they come to haunt me?
These ghosts of my past?
What if they destroy my false, familiar
sense of peace and control?
What if they make me face the me I don't want to see?

FRIEND IN DISGUISE

I am in a paralyzing state of frozen existence.
My breath takes long breaks. It's shallow, rushed, quick.

My stomach compresses hard on my abdomen
pressing against a hard knot inside.
My mind runs at the speed of light with
awful thoughts of negative fantasies.
Fear knocks on my door, enters before
I have a chance to react,
sits on the sofa with a sense of
entitlement, makes itself at home.
I hide behind the furniture not wanting
to face it; pretending it isn't there.
Then, I gather all the strength of the
Christ deep down my heart.
With Christ I stand tall, sit on the sofa, embrace fear.
After our nice little visit, she reminds me
she is not my protection, neither my destruction.
She is my friend in disguise.
She dresses like the devil
but she actually comes to awaken the Christ!

ALONE IN MY CAVE

I am acid today:
ungrateful, upset, annoyed, irritated.
I need a vacation from everything.
I lock myself in my room, do nothing,
small projects, PJ's all day.
I don't want to talk to anyone.

I don't want to hear anyone, not even the
dogs, or the air coming from the vents.
I don't want to solve anyone's problems, help anybody.
I don't even want to see anyone.
I want silence, me, the walls.
I want to relax from the world.
It's funny how I feel bad about feeling bad.
I just want to feel bad today.
Am I allowed a bad day for no reason?
It will be over tomorrow.
Just one day, away from the world, alone in my cave.

FROM AFAR

Out of the window of my hotel room I
see a beautifully crafted waterfall.
An art piece with sounds, aromas,
exotic rock formations.
It appeals to all my senses in a captivating trance.
Is this a desire to jump in or watch from afar?
Be part of the scene or admire it from a distance?
Join this art piece or stand as outside observer?

The same dilemma I have as I inhabit my human body.
The waterfall of the Spirit appeals to
my soul in captivating trance,

*yet, my body desires to stay apart from It, separated,
admire it from a distance, observe It from afar.*

ANGER

*I am your anger, your pain, your abuse,
your desire to die, to kill.
I am the one who hits, who beats,
who abuses, who destroys.
I am your darkness.
I am the one you are afraid of; the
one you pretend doesn't exist;
the one you don't love, don't pay any attention to.
The truth is that I hold the bright colors of your heart.
The truth is that I hold your inner gold, your
treasure, your key to God's kingdom.
The truth is that you only see God by seeing me first.*

CONTROL

*My body is in pain from carrying the heavy
burden of an old dying consciousness
which has perpetuated itself through
fruitless attempts to control.*

CRITICISM

There is a part of me who doesn't like me.
It criticizes me: my body, my looks, my age.
There is always something in me
that is not good enough.
This part speaks to me in many voices:
my husband's, my mom's, my kids, others.
I hear criticisms from far away.
I think they are me and I am them.
I forget who I am.
In my forgetfulness, I am somebody I don't wish to be.
I am somebody who seeks validation outside of me.
I am who I am not.
There is a part of me who needs to look
a certain way to value herself.
There is a part of me who still suffers from criticism.
There is a part of me who still waits
to be awakened anew
knowing that she is sufficient and
more than good enough.

SELF-CRITICISM

I am deep into a process of self-criticism.
I am deep into imagining what other
people think of me, or

actually, what I think they think of me.
Even if my imagination is wonderful,
even if they think well of me,
will I let them run my life?
Will I let my thinking of their thoughts run my day?
I wish things had been different, but they weren't.
I wish many things were different, but they are not.
I also know many things are better than I thought.
What the hell does it mean: better or worse or different?
Everything is as it is.
Better, worse or different is relative, temporary.
So is everything else including these words.
They are relative, temporary, useless.
My thoughts, my ideas, my life all of the
sudden, everything seems pointless,
useless…

LAMENTATION

Lamentation is to hold onto my
opinions, expectations, desires
while demanding the whole world
to follow them through.
Lamentation is to expect the world
to behave as I wish it to.
Lamentation is to victimize myself by what
I have created, promoted, allowed.

Lamentation is to live on Earth as if this
was some kind of punishment.
Lamentation is to be blind to the blessings
that are always pouring upon me.

WHAT I CREATE

I am in awe of what I create.
I see it in others very clearly.
I know it is mine to own.
I create thoughts, ideas, farfetched ones:
ideas of myself, my desires, my
children, my family, the world;
ideas that never end.
Lots of them are sad, exactly the
opposite of what I would want.
Still, I create them unknowingly, unconsciously
like a child building sand castles.
I create them mindlessly,
soon they become real in my consciousness.

STINKING THINKING

Today it was revealed to me my own weakness.
This ghost that haunts me called self-criticism.
I became so good at it

that I even anticipate the criticism
before it comes towards me.
I hear it inside my head, whether
they are even said or not.
That stinks.
That's stinking thinking!

REGRET

There is a voice deep inside of me that screams at night.
It urges for change, for life, for love.
There is a voice inside of me that is restless, impatient.
It loves the world. It's careless, free, loud.
There is a voice inside of me of
unconformity, desires, adventures.
She watches life going by.
She detaches, meditates, distracts herself.
Then, at night, she regrets.
Another day went by while she stayed behind.

A SOUL

There is this thing inside of me who wants
to be upset, get things her way.
She wants to throw a tantrum about
what she doesn't have.

She wants to be mad, blame someone else,
stand on her righteousness filled with fake power.
She wants to enjoy sexual intimacy,
look good with nice clothes,
brand-new cars just to impress.
She wants to be praised in the world; look
pretty; in a beautiful body; young, sexy.

I hear her.
I sense her.
I embrace her.

I love her unworthiness; her need for external validation.
I love her insecurity; her desire for approval, applaud.
I love her irritation; her sense of entitlement.
I love her outward focus.

I love her entirely
because through her,
beyond her,
inside her,
resides this magnificent being
of radiant light;
immeasurable beauty;
unforgettable radiance.

She is the pearl hidden inside the shell.
She is the treasure.

She is a wise woman of all times;
filled with child-like joy in a body that
transcends fashion, shapes, trends;
She is love living love.
She is the essence of everything. She is the creator.
She is the one who is aware of being
one with the Universe.

From inside the shell, hidden, invisible to
the physical eyes, she has true power,
not the power to dominate, but the power to surrender;
not the power to control, but to sacrifice;
not to judge, but to forgive;
not to do, but to be and in being then doing;
not to receive recognition, but to give praise, be Light;
not a source, but a channel;
not a person, but a soul!

PATTERNS IN CONSCIOUSNESS

It is true that what I see in my children
are the patterns in consciousness
carried by me throughout many generations of my family.
Our spiritual DNA, I see them clearly now.
I hate them deeply with a hate coming
from the origins of me.
The hate of being severed from the unity of love.

The hate of being rejected, having lost control.
The hate of realizing: "Yes, I am like
my mother, my grandfather,
my father, my aunt, my cousin, so
many others I have judged."
The hate of perpetuating, even strengthening
the undesirable patterns in my consciousness.
The hate of knowing that my hate
keeps these patterns alive.

HARD TO LOVE

Sometimes it is so hard to love.
It's so much easier to hate, blame, disgust the other,
dump on them all the darkness in me.
How I wish it was true:
they are the source of my sadness,
the cause of my upsets.
How I wish this would be as easy
as staying away from them.

WAR IS GOOD

War is good; conflict is healing.
War and conflict are venues for expression,
for letting go of anger, grief, despair, disillusion.

When such expression is received in loving acceptance,
it is transformed, transmuted, raised into loving.
This is how we are saved by Christ's wounds;
for each of his "stripes" is an expression of
anger received in loving acceptance.
Christ is the catalyst who allows anger to manifest.
His legacy of loving acceptance
allows grace to do the healing.

INERTIA

Life, all of the sudden, has been taken
by the sameness of every day
as if it requires effort to enjoy itself,
as if having fun is a chore.
There is an inertia of nothingness that
makes me walk like a zombie,
quietly, listening, observing, with no desire
to participate, to engage, to exist.

ROBBER

A robber appeared inside of me one day
to take away my joy, my laughter, my excitement.
It stole from me the desire to adventure,
to engage, to participate.

It turned colors into shades of gray.
It turned sounds into noises.
It turned my loved ones into dolls
which I enjoyed for a while, until I
tucked them away in a box.
I feel robbed of myself.
I long for the days when, filled with energy,
I wanted to drink life like a cold sweet fruit
juice on a thirsty sunny afternoon.
This robber came then left.
I am alone now in my home by
myself looking at the walls.

IS IT GRIEF?

Is it grief who is dissatisfied, who
feels unfulfilled, unworthy,
who looks to prove herself based on
material successes, achievements,
who seeks to control, look good,
who craves validation by others,
who distrusts herself,
who resists life,
who is fearful of her own light?

I ask myself
which human being has ever crossed this earthly plane
without witnessing darkness, despair, fear, terror?

GRIEF

Grief is the regretfulness of seeing life
going by without joining in,
the desperate scream of a hopeful heart,
the invisible force of death,
taking over inch by inch,
the life force of one's spirit.

STORED GRIEF

It requires courage to let me feel all
the grief that is stored in me.
Grief wants to revolt against that which is unchangeable;
wants to blame everything thereafter;
reside permanently in victimhood.

UNSPOKEN GRIEF

Grief is the unspoken, quiet, desperate powerlessness
of my inability to change what has already been.

LIFE

With everything I've lost, I've gained so much more.
With everyone that left my life, so
many more came aboard.
With every good-bye, there has
been so many welcome's.

Life is a game of losing and gaining;
letting go and letting in;
interacting and inner-acting;
grieving and enjoying.
All happening at the same time.

LONGING

There is a never ending longing that
comes with being alive:
longing for love,
longing for peace,
longing for financial stability,
longing for intimacy,
longing for a career,
longing for kids,
longing for relationship,
longing for God,
longing, more longing,

just to realize there is nothing to long for.
It is all a trap!!!!

BETRAYAL

Betrayal is the painful realization that my partner
and I are not only in different pages,
we are in different books,
written in different languages,
about different subjects.
I don't know how this happened, when or why;
or how to get back again to a unified perspective.
The task of educating one another
on where we each are
seems overwhelming enough to
make me want to run away.
Is it what we have been doing already?
Are we looking for one another, while running
desperately in opposite directions?

SPINNING CLASS

In my spinning class, I sweat in endless
circles of arduous effort,
to the sound of loud music surrounded by many people
determined to arrive nowhere.

I suddenly realize this spinning class
is much like my marriage.
In the beginning, I am energetic, excited, engaged,
filled with dreams of a great work out.
I give all of me to this bicycle to
realize it has no where to go.
The scenery doesn't change.
It is a methodical routine of sameness.
I lose stamina.
Drops of sweat fall off my face as tears fall from my eyes.
"Why am I doing this when I could be
doing many other things?" I think.
My energy drops.
The impulse to quit starts to look like an attractive option.
Yet, I hold myself to the task.
I continue deeper, stronger with each
spin of my stationary bike.
I wait anxiously for the completion,
the sense of accomplishment
that always comes after a great work out.
I am determined to overcome my own barriers,
transcend my limitations, end old patterns.
I hold onto my intention to accept what is in front of me,
to sweat, persist, endure to the end;
to use this spinning class as a vehicle to a healthier me;
to use my marriage as an angel, teacher, guide,
to the ultimate blessing of being all I can be.

LONELY

I feel so lonely inside of me.
I've had a deep conversation with my
partner but he has no idea of it.
I've put out foundational questions about
our lives but he has no clue of it.
I've spent so much energy in my
inner conversation with him,
while he sits on his desk oblivious to it all.

AFTERMATH

After the voice has spoken words of undesirable tone,
the heart has trembled with an earthquake of emotions,
the mind has shaken all thoughts like
a blender filled with food,
after all has been said, done, heard,
there is only an infinite pause of existence
which has no idea where to go or what to do.
It is the aftermath:
this long moment of shocking silence
when my body stands here
while my consciousness attempts to re-
organize itself in some rational manner.

THE BIGGEST BETRAYAL

The biggest betrayal is not a sexual
love affair outside the marriage.
It is to ignore the dreams which brought us
together into marriage in the first place.

DOING HOME

I feel betrayed
not because my partner found someone else,
but because he found something else.
In our moments of glory
in the beginning of our marriage, we
proclaimed our mission to be
"raising babies at the beach".
We declared our lives to moments of intense fun,
outdoors, near the beach, to the sound of the waves.
We agreed to dedicate our lives to raising
our babies in an uplifting energy of joy,
playfulness and togetherness.
Today, we see ourselves near the beach,
watching the most beautiful waves on Earth,
surrounded by two amazing children
who are growing faster than we can fulfill our mission.
The material components are in place,
the emotional ones are not.

Instead, we are separated
I am doing the "home";
he is doing some important mission out in the world.
I am marinating in the energy of our family;
he is spending his best hours in some office
surrounded by grateful strangers.
I am attuning to the "inherited
patterns of consciousness"
passing down to my children,
he is assisting his friends to fulfill their
mission to save the world.
Am I jealous of his endeavors?
Do I wish to be out in the world
doing the saving of others?
Do I care about the evolution of the planet
when my kids are waiting for me at home?
No, heck no...
Is it my right to ask that our mission be fulfilled
before the kids move out of the house?
Is it my place to ask for fun, joy,
playfulness, togetherness?
How can I ask him for something
that can only and truly come
voluntarily from his heart?
How can I ask him for something that
I can only truly find within?

WHAT WERE YOU THINKING?

What choices do I have when I feel betrayed?
First, realize it is my ego who feels betrayed, not my soul.
Second, remember I am not my ego.
I have feelings, but I am not my feelings.
Third, quit, give up, go away as fast as I can.
Fourth, seek, find the other person, the one I married.
Fifth, seek, find inside of me the one
who bought into this marriage,
and ask the last two: "What were you thinking?"

LONGING MADE MANIFEST

Betrayal is not the lack of love.
It is not the lack of communication.
It is not the lack.
It is not the end.

It is a call, an awakening to what could be,
to what no longer waits,
to life itself.

Betrayal is longing made manifest.

A PART OF ME

There is a part of me
that is demotivated, de-activated, desire-less.
A dreadful white noise echoing in
the background of where
excitement, discovery, engagement used to live.

INDULGENCE

I am greedy for sensations: lust, sweets, excitement.
I indulge my senses to know I am alive.
I awaken my senses for the fun of living.
I couple aliveness with sensation,
excitement with material indulgence,
enjoyment with exaggeration,
more with good; less with bad.

DO I REGRET?

Do I regret the love I shared even if it
caused pain, sorrow, tears?
Do I regret the intense moments of aliveness
even if they were short, brief, temporary?
Do I regret living my desires fully even if others
disapproved, disliked, or judged me?

Do I regret expressing my desires in actions
which others will never understand?

DESIRE

Desire is the yearning of the heart for something known,
some experience already had,
some delight already tasted which no longer is.
It is more real than fantasy, for fantasy is wishful thinking.
Desire is non-fulfillment.
Desire exists in longing, in lack, in vacuum.

DESSERTS

Somethings in life are like desserts.
They are appealing, delicious, attractive,
yet, they are followed by stomachache, indigestion.

TEMPTATION

Feeding myself from the earth is temptation.
If I resist it, I create evil.
If I succumb to it, I create illusion.

WHAT IS NO MORE

There's a thief that robs me of my self-control.
It hides in my consciousness.
All of the sudden, it catches me by surprise.

This uncontrollable beast who wants what I don't have,
longs for what is no more.

WHAT I DON'T HAVE

I sense my "wishing what I don't have"
coming back to haunt me.
It's a dark angel of mine.
I love you, appreciate you, definitely see you.
You cannot hide from me any longer.
Come on!! Join me. Tell me your secrets.

HUMAN LOVE AND DIVINE LOVE

There is human love, then there is divine love.
One is lustful, filled with desire.
It awakens me in the middle of the
night for soulful love making.
It's vibrant, young, temporary.
It's here, there, suddenly, nowhere.

It vanishes.
It's uncertain.
It's a question mark.

The other is peaceful, trustful, ever
present, cozy, reliable.
It's always here unconditionally, forever
and ever, no matter what.
It is supportive, mature, permanent,
consistent, solid, wise.
It never fails.
It surpasses anything else.
It's the exclamation point.

THE ONLY ONE

There is something unique, special,
individual, peculiar about the beloved.
In all His ordinariness, something
screams loudly "I am the only one."

EGO AND SOUL

Like everything else love too can be
experienced by the ego or by the soul.

Love by the Ego is jealous, possessive,
filled with expectations.
It holds grudges.
It is controlling, temporarily alive, conditionally present.

Love by the Soul is free, spontaneous, in
the moment, open to possibilities;
It is flowing.
It is permanently alive, unconditionally ever-present.

HUNGER

There is a hunger in me since the time of always,
which I have tried so hardly to satisfy
with total un-success.
It is a hunger that asks for food, desserts,
sauces, meat, salt, sweet.
It asks for diamonds, shoes, dresses, outfits,
beauty in the outside, expensive
smells, fancy places to go.
It asks for sex, the orgy of the body,
the surrender of the flesh
to something uncontrollable, irrational.
It asks, asks, asks.
Yet, nothing, no matter how good, how
abundant, how perfect can ever suffice.
It is a hunger that never goes away.

It subsides but doesn't disappear.
It is permanent like my breath.
It is loyal like my blood stream.
It is silent like my dreams.
It is hidden like my heart.
It is there and no-one knows, but me.
I see now, this is my spiritual hunger.
It is not looking for anything in this world,
not anything that can be touched, held with my hands,
neither anything that can be seen with my eyes of Earth.
It is a transcendental hunger
for something so much bigger, so
much better, so much more.
It is a hunger of my soul seeking to find itself.

---

13. RELATIONSHIPS

MY GRANDMOTHER

I had a dream about my grandmother.
She asked me what were the two things
that changed my life the most.
I answered: "One is my parents' divorce."
She nodded her head in agreement
validating something she already knew.
"Two is my relationship with love", I said.

KATLYN

So sweet is the love of my baby girl
who is not a baby anymore.
She is a woman in all her splendor.
She is a teenager in all her transformation.
Her love smells like flowers recently
bloomed in the spring.
Gentle, kind, uplifting.
Her smile is the sun rising in the horizon of my heart.
Infinite joy, funny jokes, interesting insights.
So full of life, full of hope, full of dreams.
The world is lucky to have her.
I am humbled to mother her.
She is my sunshine, my love, my delight.
She is forever my baby girl in my sight.

WOMAN

A woman is a mysterious universe,
She rides an emotional roller coaster every month:
high up, in altitude for awhile,
then, suddenly, bottom low with negativity, despair.
It can be disconcerting to live with such discrepancy.
It can also be a blessing.
One body, a full spectrum of emotions,
an infinite variety of experiences,
all the seasons of the year, all the faces of the moon.

*A woman is a highly evolved mechanism
designed for ultimate compassion,
unmeasurable love, unexplainable attunement.*

MY MOTHER

*Mother is beautiful, well dressed, good looking.
Her life has been long, prosperous,
her enjoyment has not;
although her life has been abundant; her joy has not.
She has had infinite ways to gladden herself,
yet she chooses to worry, fear, doubt.
Her laughter has been rare,
yet sounds to me like like the melody
of birds singing in the spring.
My mom's laughter gives me the assurance
that the universe is a friendly place.
My mom's laughter is one of the most
rewarding sounds I could ever hear.*

SAME THINGS

*I watch my daughter doing the very same things I do.
She organizes her luggage neatly,
packs a toiletry bag in her carry on,
so she can brush her teeth before boarding the plane.
She loses her patience here and there
yet, she is beautiful as a rose, sweet as mango.*

Then, I look at myself the way I carry my glasses,
the shape of my body, my nose,
the way I move, sit
and, sometimes, explode in impatient demands.
I watch myself doing the very same
things my mom has done.

MY MOM

I love my mom.
I see her caring, her loving, infinite dedication.
Behind the sacrifice, the worries, the pain,
there lies a woman of heart,
who has always been willing to give it all to her kids first.
She is the lion, the tiger, the mother bear,
who, in her motherly focus, her loving purpose,
lost sight of the fun of being alive.

ALL IS WELL

There has been moments of innocent joy
when my mom would make funny
faces, outrageous comments.
She used to make me burst into
laughter until my belly hurt.
My breathing would stop in fulfillment.
In the joy of the moment, I felt so
infinitely connected with my mom:

an eternal kind of bond beyond this
time, this world, this body.
These joyful moments with my mom
still fill my soul with delight,
with the knowing that all is well

MY MOTHER, MY QUEEN

My mother is my queen
in all her idiosyncrasies,
in all her rights, her wrongs.
She is the queen of my temple.
She sits majestically
in the throne of my heart.
I find her beautiful, elegant, confident
in her appearance,
strong, willed, determined.
She can handle anything.
She knows what she wants and won't let
others stop her from achieving it.
She looks forward to the goal.
Pragmatically, she makes it happen
with the sweat of her brow.
In her beautiful, delicate, feminine ways,
she rises above all women
as the queen of my heart!

JUST ME

As a teenager, I dreamed of having
two children, no more, no less.
One would be too lonely.
Three would be one too many.

As a young adult, I broke up many
relationships for one reason:
"He will not be a good father to my children"

I left my native country in search of finding a
better place to build a nest for my babies.
U.S.A., the home of the brave, the land of the free.
That is the place to raise my children
for free and brave, they will be.

The father had to present credentials, not only potential,
He had done it before.
"A second rodeo" he offered, I accepted.
I saw his wisdom, experience, talents,
values, determination, persuasion.
Above all, I saw a heart of gold in
magical sexual attraction.

Babies were born with golden spoons in
mansions: the best school, the best toys,
with all of the best there is to offer.

All of the sudden, I saw the fulfillment
of my own prophecies.
I connected the dots.
It absolutely had to be this way
because this has always been the way
in my dreams, intentions, actions.

The children are shining bright in health,
glory with all of the best there is.
I see their father aging, I see myself aging.
I see myself longing for mySelf,
not my children, nor the father of my children;
just mySelf, no one else, just me!

MOTHERHOOD

As a mother, I lovingly hold my
children as blank canvases.
I watch in overwhelming admiration
the choices they make,
the combination of colors they choose,
the forms they give to their lives.

I was once their womb,
lovingly holding a safe space for their bodies to form,
witnessing the miracle of physical
manifestation take shape within me.

I am now their spiritual womb,
lovingly holding a safe space for their souls to unfold,
allowing the magic of this mystical existence
to present itself through them.

PARENTHOOD

When I became a mom no one told me
I would have to be a parent.
No one told me how much I would feel
like I don't know what I am doing.
How lost I would be
when my children' actions violated
my expectations for them.
How miserable it would be to watch
them as victims of themselves.
How much I would see me in them.
No one told me parenthood is a job
for which I feel completely unprepared for.
A job that makes my ego kneel down
with limiting thoughts, projections, irrational beliefs.
A job only my Soul can take while
my ego keeps doubting.
A lifetime job of allowing my Soul to lead the way
while listening to my ego feeling completely out of place.

MY FATHER

He was handsome, tall, strong, blue-eyed,
always well dressed in his fine suits and matching ties
in perfect posture, expensive colognes.
With voice of confidence speaking other languages
unexpectedly in the middle of a dialogue.
He danced like a prince in the dark
green carpet of our home.
He behaved like a king who took the
world as his playground.
He had the majestic aura of someone
who recited poetry
in loud voice standing on the kitchen table.
He was theatrical in his mannerisms,
expansive in his heart.
He was courageous in his willingness
to expose his shortcomings,
reveal his vulnerabilities.
He was a man ahead of his time.
He stood for what he believed.
He spoke what was in his heart.
Some loved him, others hated him.
He took both: triumph and disaster
with the same dignity and glory.
The world had no time to catch up with him.
The world never gave him a Nobel prize
because the world was sleeping
while he left footsteps of gold in my soul.

MY SON

Divine Masculine in a little boy
roaring gently for the world to hear,
expanding, growing, investigating, learning, loving.
The sweetness of your innocence,
the serendipity of your laughter,
the expansion of your spirit,
the depth of your wisdom,
the infinity of your caring,
the maturity of your soul
never ceases to amaze me.
never ceases to surprise me.
Every day, I watch in awe
the miracle of the Divine Masculine
in my son.

WHAT IS A MAN?

A man is the Divine Masculine in its powerful energy
intensifying the infinity of creation
in the microcosmos of his seeds.
A man is the authority,
who serves love for the sake of love in the name of love,
because only in love a woman truly surrenders.
Only in love can the Divine Feminine
join the magic of creation.
Only in love, there is wholeness.
Only in love, laughter, spontaneity can Spirit

transform the immediacy of an instant in time
into the eternal intimacy of two in one!

MARRIAGE

In the twelve years
we've been married
we've been through
ups and downs,
high and lows.

We've been together
through good and bad,
health and sickness.

We've survived
storms and sunshines,
tears and laughters.

We've expressed ourselves truthfully
to the best of our abilities
in pleasant and unpleasant times.

We've been consistently
looking at the same direction
and that direction is love.

Through it all,
in spite of it all,
above all, and
because of it all
I still love you
now more than ever.

LOVING MYSELF FULLY

It took me a long time
to call you a husband,
to announce my love for you
forever and ever.

It took me a very long time
to see that your addictions, your
shortcomings, your misunderstandings
were actually a reflection of my own.

It has taken me an even longer time
to see that your beauty, your wisdom,
your generosity, your majesty
must also be mine.

I now know that you are my husband
not because society calls you so,
but because I chose you to be my mirror
to show me the truth,

all of the truth,
about me
and, in your loving arms,
learn to love myself
fully.

MY PARTNER

I have spent twelve years of my marriage
calling for love,
calling for connection,
calling for fun.

I have spent twelve years of my marriage
wishing my partners's volition
would make him stay home,
enjoy the serendipitous moment.

I have spent twelve years of my marriage
wondering why he wakes up at 5 am every morning,
why he leaves early in the day
only to come back in the evening;
why he is so busy on the weekends;
and emotionally away so often?

I have spent twelve years of my marriage
reflecting upon the dreadful possibility
that my partner is a reflection of me.

As a result, I built a routine of intense inner work,
quietude, meditation, connection with mySelf.
I love the world I built for myself,
and sometimes, it feels like
my partner does not fit in it any more.

ADDICTION

Loving a man with addiction is like eating
a candy with the wrapping still on;
the sweetness is so close yet I can't quite taste it;
he is present yet not entirely here.
It is like dying of thirst in front of the ocean.
A permanent frustration that life is not quite there for me,
not quite reachable,
not quite achievable,
not quite satisfiable.
I am in love with someone with
prison bars in between us.
I can never quite fully indulge in him,
for there is a part of him
who is numbed out,
checked out,
dying out
from the love
waiting
patiently
right

in
front
of
his
very
eyes.

MY PLAYGROUND
A delicious anticipation.
An opening in my heart.
An awakening of my soul.
An invitation to play, join this Earth in its glory.
Make it my playground.
Be a kid again.
All is possible.
My imagination is about to become my reality.

MY HOME
I've cradled you,
held you tight, my darling.
I've protected your body, your soul, your dreams.
I've kept you safe day and night
to play, laugh, dream, cry, grow, learn,
to become a woman and fly.

I've held strength in moments of weakness.
I've held tenderness in moments of joy.
No matter what, I've held you.
I've watched you grow
from the cradle to the world,
from my walls to the oceans, continents abroad.

I've held you, protected you
so that you could spread far, wide
the same unconditional loving arms
which I cradled you by.

LAST DAY OF CHILDHOOD

It was early morning, a regular beautiful weekend.
My parents gathered us into a meeting.
"What? A meeting? What for?" I thought.
"We've never had a family meeting
before. What is this all about?"

In our living room, three kids - my older
brother, my younger sister, I - sat down
on the large couch with orange and brown stripes,
the dark green carpet underneath us.
Our young legs were too short to even reach the floor.
Our feet hung on the edge of the couch,

while our hearts hung on the suspense
of this mysterious meeting.

Will we get a gift? Buy a new car?
Go on a trip? Get a puppy?
An infinitude of possibilities crossed
my innocent, lively mind.

I looked at my older brother, my younger sister.
Their big green eyes sparkled with a
mixture of excitement and doubt.
They too wished it was something good but,
we all recognized the morbid sense in the air.

My parents looked dreadful, dull.
My mom had been crying.
"Did anyone die?" I thought.

"We are getting divorced", they said.
"Do you want to live with mom or dad?"

Seriously?
Did they expect us, kids, to provide them
with an answer they couldn't find?
I just cried, a deep sad cry like I had never cried before.
What else could a child do or say?

An avalanche of fear invaded my mind:
"How would we survive?
Where would daddy live?
How could we live without him?
Do I want to go with daddy or stay with mommy?"
I just wanted to run away.
And, so I did.

I marched out of our home, down the busy
city streets for quite a long while.
I am not sure how my parents let me
leave the house on my own.
I was wearing my favorite outfit:
a baby blue sleeveless shirt with navy and
white embroidery on the shoulders,
a navy sweatpants with two white stripes
going down on each side of my legs.

I walked by myself - me and my outfit -
amongst the cars, people, houses.
I was on my own.
For the first time, I felt like I was on my own.
I was alone. I felt completely alone.
"I better take care of myself 'cause
no one else will," I thought.

Childhood, whatever that meant, was no more.
Just me and my outfit facing life yet to come.

KARMA

How is it that I see my karma* reflected
back to me in my children?
How is it that I want to correct them, control
them, change them, instead of me?

MY EVIL

How can I still attempt to change what I don't like in me
by trying to change my daughter when she acts like me?

How is it that I see my evil reflected back
to me in my daughter's actions
and I try to change her by applying my evil back to her?

RELATIONSHIPS

Relationships are not to make me happy
but to make me conscious.
It is in my closest relationships that I
find the strongest vortex of love
pulling out most of my discomforts,
triggers, disturbances.
I watch myself turning, twisting in a knot inside.

I watch myself feeling defeated under
a dark cloud of hopelessness.
In this dreadful, dull moment of total non-
resistance, surrendering, fatal allowing,
there comes love in a flash
running through the middle of this
vortex of precious garbage,
pushing away the darkness:
the magic of a holy instant of miraculous ordinariness.
I ask myself: "what was that?"
I hear inside: "It's love! It's grace! It's life!"
That's what relationships are for...

INTEGRATING TRAUMA

I finally remember what I had forgotten: the abuse!

The abuser didn't know, couldn't see,
or was blind to the abuse.
The abuser stole the abused's ability
to see the abuse, also.
The abuse became normal, the ways things were.
It remained 'normal', hidden until
the abused saw it coming back
in their own reactions later in life.
Disproportionate reactivity.

Where did that come from?
From the hidden dark silence of the abuse.

The abused remained quiet for so long
because the abused couldn't really see the abuse.
The abused took in the abuse as part of themselves.
The abused integrated the abuse as who they were,
as what they lived with, and survived.

So, if the abused survived, and is still standing,
then the abuse wasn't so, right?!?
The mind of the abused wants so
badly to move past the abuse,
that it convinces itself that the best
place for abuse is in the silence.

The mind of the abused pushes the abuse
away to let the past be in the past;
to move forward;
to keep strong;
to survive.

The abused wants to forget the abuse.
Then, something seemingly unrelated happens;
and the abused reacts with an impulse
that had been forgotten;
with the energy of something that had
been repressed for a long time.

Upon this energetic implosion,
the abused, then, abuses themselves.
The abused criticizes, judges and
condemns themselves and others.

This is when the abused becomes the abuser.
This is when the abuse takes the center
force of motivation in the abused.
This is when the abused continues the
abuse, as the abuser, unconsciously...

Until the abused stops, reflects, observes,
finally receives the abuse with
neutrality and acceptance,
No blame,
No shame,
Simply recognizing the energetic progression of what is.

In this moment of deep realization,
there is no longer the abuse, the
abuser, nor the abused.
There is only unbearable compassion,
Unbearable acceptance,
Unbearable embrace,
Unbearable grace.
The visceral knowing that the abuse is the Light,
which must be brought forward, spoken about,
be honored, felt, expressed constructively,

through the compassion, acceptance,
embrace, grace that it entails.

The 'peace that surpasses
understanding' comes present,
with higher levels of vibratory awareness.

There is no longer abuse, abused and abuser.
There is only awareness,
the openness and willingness to dive even further
into the merciful ocean of awareness,
which is constant,
which is nothing and no-thing,
which is anything, everything and all things,
which is!

---

14. TRANSCENDING MY MASKS

COURAGE

"It takes courage to become who I truly
am," I hear someone say to me.
Courage to let go of the masks that
bind me to nothing, nowhere.
Courage to take a step towards the outrageous,
to dare, to live, to be alive again.

Courage to not allow my weaknesses to
kill me while I am still breathing.

SHEDDING

I am shedding the layers of me that no longer fit.
I am shedding my misconceptions,
judgments, irrational beliefs.
I am shedding my attachments,
admirations, goals, objectives.
I am shedding so much there may be
nothing left in the end to tell the story.

IN THE MIDST

In the midst of what I could never imagine of,
I found myself to be what I never thought I could be.

BRAZIL AND ME

I am moved by the current situation in Brazil.
The unveiling of mass corruption, lies,
scandals in the government,
which robs people not only of their money,
but also of their hope, their lives,
their trust, joy, innocence.

I am moved because, as a Brazilian,
I experience the same pain of
transformation as my motherland.

In my life too, the mass of deep lies,
corruption, scandals have finally unveiled.
The pain of looking at what it really is,
rather than what I wished it was,
or what I pretended it to be.

The courage to pull up to the light
the deeply buried roots of
many generations of limiting beliefs,
irrational perspectives,
a form of playing pretend, living the lie of a pleasant life,
rather than the pain of an unpleasant truth.

Accepting the part of me which claimed:
"they didn't rob too much;" or
"they robbed but they did something for me;"
and in doing so,
kept choosing the same leaders, the same ways,
the same attitude, the same perspective
in the hope that things would change.

Like Brazil, I too am facing my own insanity:
which insists in doing the same things over and over
wishing to obtain different results.

I too am facing the harsh truths which
I have avoided for so long,
perhaps for many generations in my family's heritage;
perhaps, even many lifetimes.

This is the Golden Age for me and,
and maybe for Brazil.
The time to be lost in finding myself.
The courage to open up the Pandora box,
face my lies, my scandals, my own inner corruption;
look at my un-rightable wrongs.

Like the prodigal son who arrived back home,
I celebrate the fact that I am back
home again, in the Light.
There are no longer monsters hidden in
the dark, afraid of coming out.
It is all revealed. All of me.
The truth of me. All parts of me.

And, I can still say to myself, as I do to my country,
"I know everything but I love you."

TIRED
I am tired of sustaining fear as the
foundation for my decision making;

sustaining rejection as the basis
for my searching for love;
sustaining outside validation as the
evidence of my worthiness;
sustaining compliance as the
condition for my acceptance;
sustaining beauty as the requirement for my inclusion;
sustaining money as the foundation for my safety;
sustaining sex as the vehicle for my release;
sustaining power as the path to influence;
sustaining "againstness" as the method for change;
sustaining death as a way of living.

EYE OF A NEEDLE

I have infinite tasks but my heart is not there.
I have infinite opportunities but my soul is single.
I have so much but my calling is narrow.
I am going through the eye of a needle,
shedding away what is not me.

ZOMBIE

Most of the time, I have no idea what I am saying or why.
Most of the time, I am distracted with
ridiculous tasks that never end.
Most of the time, I am a zombie in paradise.

IF I HAD NOTHING TO DO

Ever since I was a child
I always had so much to do.
I used to wonder what adults meant when they said:
"It is so easy to be a child!"
"They wouldn't say that if they knew all I have to do,"
I secretly thought to myself.
My list of to do's flew down my
consciousness like Niagara Falls.
It still does.
I carry a long useless list of to do's
assigned from me to myself.
Perhaps, watching my mother always so "busy,"
I programmed myself to belief that to live is to be busy.
Under that standard, I have been living well, really well.

I wonder now:
What is my passion?
What lights up the fire of my heart?
What would I be if I didn't have so much to do?
What would I do as a natural consequence of my being?
What would I soulfully be drawn into?
What would my soul direct me to do
if my mind wasn't so busy
filling up every hour of my day?
What would the schedule of my soul look like?
What would I be if I had nothing to do?

15. TRANSMUTATION*:
THE GRACE OF CHRIST*

ANTI-CHRIST

Anti-Christ is that which blocks me
from Christ Consciousness.
It may be an explosion, a pain, a disease of some kind
which has the potential to liberate me from
whatever keeps me away from Christ.
It is the overcoming of the Anti-christ that
brings me into oneness with Christ.
In that sense, the Anti-christ does Christ a service
Through the Anti-christ, I find Christ.

CHRIST'S HOLY FREQUENCY

I woke up in the middle of the night
sweating a cold sweat
like a rain of ice falling on boiling water.
I opened my eyes to find the room
spinning fast around me
as if I was on a wild tea cup ride.
If I closed my eyes, the dizziness worsened.
If I opened my eyes, the dizziness was scarier.
I laid there welcoming death, wondering
whether to call for help.

"Emergency", I cried silently inside.
As an immediate answer to my call,
a violent avalanche of waste came from inside of me
rushing out like a tsunami of sewage
exploding out of my cold sweaty body
with barely any time to run to the bathroom.
My only choice was to surrender, allow the
wisdom of my body to take charge.
My entire being was activated in this
clearing action from inside out
which surpassed any sense of control my
conscious mind attempted to have.
Everything I could no longer stomach,
everything I could no longer hold inside
erupted out of me like a mad volcano.
My resistance was torn open.
The gates of my illusion of control were pushed apart.
There I stood, naked, vulnerable,
facing the rotten smell of all the garbage I kept inside:
the tight schedule of kids, school, homework, dinner...
violin, karate, piano, dentist appointments...
all the "must do's" I tried so hard to keep alive
just because, they were supposed to be,
just because, who knows why...
"Why?" I asked myself in this dreadful moment
of standing face-to-face with the
stinky rotten parts of me.

Suddenly, I realized in my effort to do
everything right, all was going wrong;
in my effort to do what it was supposed
of me, I was left forgotten;
in my effort to keep everything
together, I was breaking apart,
in my effort to keep going, I was killing the preciousness,
the bliss of each unscheduled moment.

I now breathe consciously, lightly,
a breath that feels as sweet, gentle as the breath of God.
Today, God made a storm in my insides.
My soul pushed out of this body temple
all of that which I resisted looking at,
which was no longer serving me,
which I was afraid to face.
Christ has poured His grace upon me.
The Holy Spirit baptized my cells, my DNA.
My body temple has been blessed
with Christ's Holy frequency.

SOME DAYS
Some days are filled with sunshine
even when it's overcast;
Some days are filled with laughter even
when nothing is particularly funny;
Some days are so peaceful even in the midst of chaos;

Some days are the best even when ordinary;
Some days are so filled with loving
just because....

THE KINGDOM WITHIN

He came to show us unconditional loving.
The old laws were engraved in his
heart with bloody letters.
For Him, the laws are made for the
inner, not the outer, world.
They are guidelines for a loving heart.
They are about inner obedience, true love inside out.
They are not parameters upon which to judge.
They are the source of all forgivenesses,
the cessation of all judgments.
Out in the world, laws are surely violated.
In fact, they were violated against His
very being, His holy body.
Forgive them, seventy times seven,
as He demonstrated in flesh and blood when crucified.
The Kingdom of Heaven has never
been out in this world,
it has always been within.

A WALK WITH CHRIST

Christ took me for a walk in a dark forest.
He showed me an old big wooden medieval
door hidden under the shadow of a tree.
Christ pointed to the dark door, the door
fell down gently forming a bridge over a
mysterious abyss of darkness and mist.
It looked scary, unfriendly, unsafe.
Christ said to me in a soft but strong
voice: "Cross it, my dear".
I paused, wondered:
"why would a loving Christ ask me to cross
such a scary bridge in the dark alone?"
Then, I remembered the same loving Christ
also asked Peter to walk on water
which he did, and then failed with
his first thought of doubt.
I heard Christ asking, as he asked
Peter: "Where is your faith?".
I gathered all my courage, my faith.
I kept my eyes on the Christ, on the
Lord, on His comforting promise.
I crossed that scary bridge, seemingly alone
with trembled steps and a faithful heart.
On the other side, when I arrived,
Christ greeted me.
Christ reminded me fear and doubt weren't real.

They were but a pretense of my
mind designed to make me
gather all my faith to walk towards the
Christ, who has never left me.

WASTE

Jesus, the Christ was crucified for my sins.
Through his wounds, I am healed.
Through his resurrection, I receive the Holy Spirit.
Through his way, I have grace.
What a waste his life would be if I reject to
reside in that place of loving within
which he has prepared for me.

16. DIVINE INTIMACY

WHEN I AM IN YOU

My soul is the source of my desire.
It is the source of life, the source of love.
You awaken my soul,
reactivate the dormant life force,
pulsate in my blood with every breath.
An avalanche of energy, a vortex of universal power
come upon me when I am in You.

IN THE NOW

Where is my creativity, my words to be expressed?
There is so much inside of me, yet
nothing comes down to this paper.
There is afflictions, doubts, fear, anxiety.
I don't identify with them anymore.
There is love, sacrifice, forgiveness.
They are instantaneous relief, relaxation.
Then, there is now.
A big great infinite now with no words to describe,
no expression to write, nothing to say or do.
Just be, in the now!

MORE THAN I COULD BE

Love has a way of making me abdicate of myself,
sacrifice myself, lose myself,
know the me who is unplanned,
who is devoted to life,
who is willing to give it all, do it all, sacrifice it all,
the me who is so filled with love
that doesn't measure sacrifices neither count scores,
the me who I never knew I was,
the me who I never knew I could be,
the me who is much more than I ever thought to be.

ALIVENESS

My heart is a garden where birds
sing a sweet melody of joy;
the trees dance in the wind like
ballerinas in tutu dresses.
There is peace in my heart enveloped
by the joy of being alive.
There is aliveness in my being.
I am present to the plenitude inside of me.
I am awaken to the infinite of what is
as if I had just been born.

GARDEN OF EDEN

Today, I spent my day at the Garden of Eden
Today, I confirm the Garden of Eden
is alive, present, available
in its energetic form as a potential
waiting to be tapped into.
Today, I experienced paradise in my
relationships with myself, others, the world,
not because everything was perfect
as one might imagine,
but because everything was fluid, natural, spontaneous.
Everything was a discovery, an
allowing, a sweet surrender.

A BOAT CALLED LOVE

In each heartbeat, God reminds me
I float in a boat called "Love,"
on a river named "Conspiring in my Favor,"
making stops at "My Highest Good" stations.

There is nothing to like or dislike, agree or disagree.
There is only what is.
There is only curiosity, openness, trust.
Knowing that the perfect order of this
Universe is leading my life.
This place has been prepared for me.
My inheritance.
My Garden of Eden which has
always been, has never left.
I now claim, explore, discover it as a child of God
who has arrived Home!

MENOPAUSE

It is the part of me that was hidden inside,
perhaps under criticism, judgments, attacks;
perhaps ashamed, suppressed,
condemned, depressed.
This part of me now comes up to the surface
in hot flashes, insomnia, introspection.
My hair is thinner, and my wisdom is deeper.

My skin is looser, and my inner core is stronger.
My eyesight is poorer, and my inner senses are rich.
My sexual intercourse is infrequent, and
my supra-sexuality* is constant.
My sense of self in this physical world is changed
and my sense of self in oneness with
this universe is just born.

BATH BOMB

My bath bomb in blue, yellow, pink,
white melts slowly in bath water,
exhaling a sensuous, penetrating perfume
that makes me feel worthy.
The busy days moving into a new house,
managing everyone's feelings
are all worthy now
because of this royal aroma embracing my
body in the delicious warmth of my bath.

Out of the window, the big leaves of
the palm tree dance freely
to the melody of the wind
on a backstage of the light blue sky.

The bath bomb is the same color
scheme as our new home.

I see old thoughts, emotions, memories
melting away in my bathwater
like bubbles of time washed off of me.

I am more grateful, more aware, more
solid, more patient, more consistent,
and above all, more Me than ever before.

ORGASM
It is my soul rising above my illusions,
manifesting magnificently upon my mundane existence,
making me see everything through
the lenses of the divine,
turning all I see into ordinary miracles
as if the whole world is having an orgasm with me.

SERVICE
My heart feels full.
God made use of me today in service, in
balance, in beauty, in Light, in humility.
Please God hold my ego in Your infinite loving
so it may always know the comfort of your arms,
so it may always surrender to Your guidance,
so it may always follow Your Lead,

so that it may always submit to You
as the Commander-in-Chief
of my army of personalities.

SAME VASE

I woke up today like a flower in the same
vase, same soil, same world,
yet, nothing else is the same.
My petals opened up.
The view is vast like I had never seen before.

EXPANSION

How does God expand if It's already all-encompassing?
God expands through me, as me, in me
with each smile, each tear, each breath.
God never ceases to expand.

RHYTHM

There is a rhythm to my rhythm.
I take care of myself. I feel amazing.
I go into a drought. I forget myself in
the bottom of my priorities.
I feel bad. I take care of myself again.
I am disciplined in my spiritual practice.
I see goodness in the presence of the Lord.

I relax, become over-confident.
Negativity creeps upon me.
I lose myself. I find myself.
Like a song, the melody intensifies;
then it slows down again.
Like the breath, it comes in, then goes out.
Like the universe, the seasons, the weather patterns.
There is a universal rhythm in me.

LUXURIOUS UNIVERSE

I am not materialistic, or at least, I like
to think so, yet I enjoy luxury,
The beauty, politeness, cleanliness which
comes with luxury reflect back to me
the perfection of our Universe, the
majestic order of all there is.
There is a place for everything, everything has its place.
There is magnificence, organization in the night sky,
in outer space, the solar system, the galaxies,
It is perfection beyond comprehension.
This is indeed a luxurious universe!

ORCHID IN A POT

I woke up this morning with words dancing in my head
like ballerinas in tutu on a stage.
"Sobriety", I hear.

"Forgiveness, love, trust".
"Let life undo me".
Words twist and turn in my head in a gentle dance
which wakes me up from my sleep,
takes me out of my ego's bed,
to step on the ground underneath me
as if I know what I am doing.

What if God sent me to Earth to show me what Love is?
What if everything in this world is a
demonstration of divine love?
What if my intelligence is best used in
observation, factual description
as if I was noticing an orchid in a pot?
What if God gave me life, just like an orchid in a pot,
then told me to observe it attentively,
so I could know what Love is?
What if I can not learn love in a book, just
like I can't drink water by reading H2O?

I want to drink the world like a glass of
cold water on a sunny hot day.
hydrating my consciousness with
the experience of true love.

LIFE

Life is a constant change from what was to what
is yet to be while caught in the middle.

GOD KNOWS BEST

I could end this day wishing my day
had been this or that; or
I could go to bed without this or that; or
it could have been this or that.
What are my wishes good for in the ignorant
perspective I have of my highest good?
I much rather end this day holding that God knows best!

PLEASE DON'T LET ME BE MISUNDERSTOOD

"I am just a soul whose intentions are good.
Come on, please, don't let me be misunderstood,"
sang the voice on the radio of my car in loud volume.
Parked in front of the grocery store,
in the middle of an argument.
I had been completely misunderstood.
I heard his blames on me, his criticisms of me.
In the midst of this dreadful controversy,
he demanded an answer from me.
Quietly, I stayed on the driver seat
with the door half open,
the pavement below as an ocean of darkness,

listening to this song I had enjoyed very
much in my adolescence in Brazil,
but could never decipher the words
until this strange moment many decades later,
when these fatal words appeared as
clear as the blue sky above me.
They were exactly the words I wanted to sing to him.
Spirit was playing a prank on me.
Was this the movie of my life playing a divinely
orchestrated background soundtrack?
Laughter came up from deep inside of me.
Spirit had set it all up just perfectly.
So that I would know It is always watching over me.

THE MEANING OF LOVE

I sit quietly, waiting for life to tell
me what it intends for me.
It's nothing glamorous nor big.
It's to bring the meaning of love to
what is right in front of me.

BEAUTIFULLY MUNDANE

We sat down to talk for hours.
I spoke freely, openly.
He held in gentle, loving attention.

We talked about the kids, the future, the
house, our experiences, ourselves.
We went to bed with a simple good night hug.
We woke up next morning in an intimate embrace.
Nothing extraordinary yet so extra ordinary.
How many miracles lie in the ordinariness of life?
What a profound sense of love
resides in a mundane breath.
How beautiful is the mundane!

CHRISTMAS TIME
It's Christmas time.
We put up the tree as a family for the first time ever.
Our daughter plays soft violin in the background,
Our son giggles, dances around.
The delicious aroma of a fresh cooked
meal is still floating in the air.
The sparkle of each ornament lightens
up a flame of love in my heart.
Sweet evening like no other I have ever experienced.

JOY
I don't know where this joy comes from.
Whether is from a sense of freedom
that comes after the storm.
I cried my grievances.

I felt sorry for myself.
I shared my losses.
I heard my pain.
It now has left a sense of ecstasy, freedom
from which words just flow,
hopping up and down onto this paper like a bunny
delivering chocolate eggs on Easter!

TERROR IN BELGIUM
There was terror in Belgium today.
Tragic news of death, horror.
Which I heard about while sitting on a
pool chair of a five star resort.
It seems so surreal, so impossible,
so many people dying
while I sit comfortably in vacation land.

May my overflow of joy be overreaching enough
to bring some energy of peace, harmony
to the ones affected by these horrible news.

May the pain and hardship of this
moment assist each one of us
to faithfully hold on to a higher intelligence,
although not understood,
still perfectly designed.

REGULAR DAY

I don't have much to say on this just regular day.
I could go into my worries which are unnecessary.
I could go into my wishes which are
willful, expectation builders.
I could go into nothingness which
is kind, sweet, accepting.
In this nothingness, I actually feel complete
with nothing to change or fix;
nothing to wish for,
other than to keep it quiet, calm,
conscious for as long as it lasts.

EASTER

I have a deep desire to say: "I Love you"
to those who can not understand me,
who judge me, criticize me,
the ones who yell at me, curse me,
the ones who keep distance from me.
I have a deep desire to tell them how much I love them,
understand them, hear them.
I have a deep desire to appreciate
them because they teach me
with every thought, every memory
to forgive more,
to renew again,
to move further,

to resurrect out of what was into the what is in the now.
New life!
New perspective!
Newness!!
It's Easter in my soul today and every day forever more.

CONSCIOUSNESS

The consciousness of wrong looks at the
wrongness of everything to change it.
The consciousness of beauty looks at the
beauty of everything to appreciate it.
The consciousness of God looks at the
goodness of everything to bless it.
All of them are available to me at every moment.

ALREADY

There was a time when I felt as a prisoner
of others, of circumstances, situations.
A prisoner of my past, my story, my wishes.
Then, I woke up. I discovered I was
only a prisoner of myself:
my thoughts, my misinterpretations, my illusions,
my sense of lack, my misguided consciousness.

I loved them fully. I washed them off.
After I was all done, they greeted me
with a blessing I will keep forever.
The blessing of unconditionality,
wholeness, communion.

I have once been a prisoner scattered in million pieces.
Today, I am a bird flying free in the
sky of my imagination.
I am already whole. I am already
light. I am already complete.
I am already what I wish to be.

GOD

Sometimes, life needs a pause,
a shift in gear, a change of pace.
There is a turn, a bifurcation ahead.
I slow down, give a closer look, turn.
It's a new road, new path, new destination.
Eons of ethers are with me.
My time has come to make this turn.
I am on my way to God.
God? What is God?
Where is God? Is God a destination?
Oops....
God is the journey, also the destination.

God is the way, also the turn, the gear
shifting, the road, the eons of ethers.
God is all.
I am in God. God is in me.
I am God. God is me.
Where am I going?
Not sure. Don't care, do I?
No, as long as God and I are one.

ABOVE ALL, LOVE

Love what you like and what you don't.
Love what you do and what you don't.
Love who you are and who you think you are not.
Love the good and the bad;
the right and the wrong;
the beautiful and the ugly.

Love, not because you agree, but because you care.
Let Love show you what to do and,
most importantly, how to be.
Love may guide you to go or stay;
be silent or loud;
be humble or bold.

Love may take you in opposite
directions so you recognize

Love is in you, as you and through you.
Love is a place inside you go to.

When you find Love within,
no matter what you live through,
you live it fully,
because you use life for
learning, growth, upliftment, expansion and enthusiasm.

When you don't find Love within,
no matter how great life may be,
you live it incompletely,
because part of you seeks to find Love out in the world.

Go on, darling,
Let life show you Love and
Let Love show you life,
so that you may know
the Light, the Beauty and the Wholeness
you have always been.

GLOSSARY[1]

Attunement. A inner state of oneness or *at-one-ment* with oneself.

Christ Consciousness. A universal consciousness of pure Spirit. Exists within each person through the Soul.

Consciousness. Consciousness is the state or quality of awareness, or, of being aware of an external object or something within oneself.

Deborah Martinez. The facilitator of the PTS Doctor of Spiritual Science (DSS) program.

Divine. God, Supreme Intelligence, Creator

Divine Intimacy. The deepest level of revelation I can experience with myself in loving acceptance for all the parts of my consciousness. The ability to lovingly recognize, accept, and understand the patterns, beliefs, and conceptions that form the matrixes of my consciousness.

---

[1] John-Roger, D.S.S. 2006. *Fulfilling Your Spiritual Promise.* Mandeville Press, where most definitions in the Glossary are taken from.

Divine Feminine. The feminine principle in the universe which expresses itself in every creative act together with the Divine Masculine. The feminine principle expresses the receptive movement of taking in and nurturing. In distortion, the feminine principle turns from loving receptivity and nurturing to grasping, grabbing, stealing, holding tight, catching, and taking without letting go.[2]

Divine Masculine. The masculine principle in the universe which expresses itself in every creative act together with the Divine Feminine. The masculine principle expresses the outgoing movement of reaching, giving, acting, initiating, asserting. In distortion and negativity, the masculine principle manifests as hostile aggression, hitting rather than giving and reaching.[3]

Doctorate of Spiritual Sciences (DSS). The PTS Doctor of Spiritual Science (DSS) program is essentially designed to get you on very friendly terms with yourself. You get to sit down and meet yourself, face-to-face. It's set up so you can be conscious in all ways and on all levels of yourself. So, a whole lot is going on to release you from

---

[2] Eva Pierrakos and Judith Saly. 1993,2002. *Creating Union. The essence of Intimate Relationship.* The Pathwork Foundation Inc. Page 157

[3] Eva Pierrakos and Judith Saly. 1993,2002. *Creating Union. The essence of Intimate Relationship.* The Pathwork Foundation Inc. Page 157

limitations: references that don't work for you, things that you've created that no longer serve you.

Drs. Ron and Mary Hulnick. The President and Chief Academic Director of the University of Santa Monica

Ego. A personality. The part of the a consciousness which experiences and reacts to the world from a dualistic perspective, varying in a spectrum of positive to negative charge.

God. Supreme Intelligence of Creation. Absolute unity of everything there is.

Golden Thread. A line of high vibratory energy connecting the the highest chakras with God.

Grace of Christ. "With the Soul, hope springs eternal and that hope is being generated through grace. When you enter into grace, you walk through your life in great security and confidence, knowing that you are living God's perfection every moment." John Morton, Loving Each Day. www.msia.org

High Self. The self that functions as one's spiritual guardian, directing the conscious self towards those experiences that are for one's greatest spiritual progression. It has knowledge of the destiny pattern agreed upon before embodiment.

John Morton. John Morton inspires and educates people around the world on the teachings of the spiritual heart and recognizing the blessings in all situations. He serves as Spiritual Director of MSIA, anchors the Mystical Traveler Consciousness and guides those on the path of Soul Transcendence. John is an accomplished author, masterful facilitator, and loving friend to all.

John-Roger (J-R). The founder of the Movement of Spiritual Inner Awareness. For over 50 years, John-Roger devoted his life to being a Wayshower for others to find Spirit within themselves and demonstrate how to live life in greater loving, happiness, and peace. J-R's humor, joy, and unconditional loving embraced and touched people around the planet. His good works continue on, guiding those studying the path of Soul Transcendence, which is becoming aware of oneself as a Soul and as one with God, not as a theory but as a living reality.

Karma. The law of cause and effect; as you sow, so you shall reap. The responsibility of each person for his or her actions. The law that directs and sometimes dominates a being's physical existence.

Light. The energy of Spirit that pervades all realms of existence. Also refers to the Light of the Holy Spirit.

Movement of Spiritual Inner Awareness (MSIA). An organization whose major focus is to bring people into an awareness of Soul Transcendence, which is becoming aware of yourself as a Soul and as one with God. John-Roger is the founder. www.msia.org

Traveler or Mystical Traveler Consciousness. A high vibratory consciousness of love emanated directly from God and anchored as a potential in everyone through the Soul. The Mystical Traveler Consciousness is freedom. It expresses freedom and gives freedom. Its nature is love, joy, and upliftment. It brings health, wealth, and happiness on the physical level, calm to the emotional level, peace to the mental level, ability to the unconscious level, and the fulfillment of all the dreams to the spiritual level. It's important to remember that the Traveler is not something separate from you. It's a consciousness that is within each person. Each person's inner spiritual journey is an awakening to the Traveler on all levels, up into the very heart of God. To get an idea of how the Traveler works with people, you could think of climbing a mountain, say Mount Everest. If reaching the top of it were your goal, you might want to climb with the assistance, suggestions, encouragement, and guidance of someone who has already climbed it and knows the way. Similarly, the Traveler Consciousness is one who knows the way "up the mountain" to the Soul level and above, who can guide and assist you spiritually. Still, though, the climb is always yours. You are the one who does it.

Peace Theological Seminary & College of Philosophy (PTS). Founded in 1977 by Dr. John-Roger, Peace Theological Seminary & College of Philosophy (or simply "PTS") offers experiential education on practical spirituality. PTS is the educational arm of the Movement of Spiritual Inner Awareness (MSIA), which main focus is to support students with learning the lessons of the physical and spiritual worlds. www.ptswisdom.org

Robbie Burt. Reader and graduate of the Doctorate of Spiritual Psychology (DSS)

Soul. The extension of God individualized within each human being. The basic element of human existence, forever connected to God. The indwelling Christ, the God within.

Spirit. See also 'Soul.' The representative of God in each being and on Earth.

Spiritual DNA. Just as our biological DNA transmits inheritances of physical characteristics from the parents to the child, the Spiritual DNA transmits the legacy of the parents' evolving consciousness to the child.

Spiritual Exercises (S.E.'s). Chanting the Hu, the Ani-Hu, or one's initiation tone. An active technique of bypassing the mind and emotions by using a spiritual tone to connect to the Sound Current. Assists a person in breaking through the illusions of the lower levels and eventually moving into Soul consciousness.

Spiritual Heart. The inner consciousness which awakens humans to their connection with the Divine, providing opportunities for awareness of one's spiritual loving nature.

Spiritualize. To become more deeply connected with one's spiritual essence and nature.

Tithe. An offering to God of something valuable.

Transmutation. The history of the word teaches that from Old French, *transmutation* (12c.), from Late Latin *transmutationem* (nominative *transmutatio*) means "a change, shift." Also, from the verb in Latin *transmutare which means* "change from one condition to another".

Traveler or Traveler Consciousness. (see Mystical Traveler Consciousness)

Universe. A term that encompass everything there is animate and inanimate, alive or not, visible or not, physical or not. A catch all term for everything there is.

University of Santa Monica. Formerly known as Koh-e-nor University, was founded in March of 1976 in Los Angeles. The inspiration for the University came from its Founder, distinguished educator, internationally known lecturer, and best-selling author, John-Roger. His vision was of a graduate school of the highest caliber, where students across the globe could come learn how to live in this world, be in the here and now, and be involved in the unique process of spiritualizing themselves. www.universityofsantamonica.edu

REFERENCE LIST

Anthony William. 2015. *Medical Medium. Secrets Behind Chronic and Mystery Illness and How to Finally Heal.* Hay House Inc.

Bruce Lipton, Ph.D. 2005. *The Biology of Belief. Unleashing the Power of Consciousness, Matter & Miracles.* Mountain of Love / Elite Books

Carey Ellen Walsh. 2000. *Exquisite Desire. Religion, the Erotic, and the Song of Songs.* Augsburg Fortress

Christiane Northrup, M.D. 2006. *Women's Bodies. Women's Wisdom. Creating Physical And Emotional Health and Healing.* Bantam Books

Doreen Virtue and Becky Black. 2001 *Eating In The Light. Making the Switch to Veganism on Your Spiritual Path.* Hay House Inc.

Eva Pierrakos. 1999. *Compulsion to Recreate Childhood Hurts.* The Pathwork Foundation (Pathwork Guide Lecture. No 73. An Unedited Lecture. November 11, 1960).

Eva Pierrakos. 1999. *Mobility In Relaxation; Suffering Through Attachment Of Life For To Negative Situations.* The Pathwork Foundation (Pathwork Guide Lecture No. 135. An Unedited Lecture. June 25, 1965).

Eva Pierrakos & Donovan Thesenga. 1997. Surrender to God Within. Pathwork Press

Eva Pierrakos and Judith Saly. 1993,2002. *Creating Union. The essence of Intimate Relationship.* The Pathwork Foundation Inc.

Hazel Henderson, Jean Houston, Barbara Marx Hubbard edited by Barbara Delaney. 2007. *The Power of Yin. Celebrating Female Consciousness.* Cosimo. Chapter XIII.

Heinz R. Pagels. 1982. *The Cosmic Code. Quantum Physics as the Language of Nature* Bantam Books, Inc.

H Ronald Hulnick, Ph.D. and Mary R. Hulnick, Ph.D. 2010. *Loyalty to Your Soul. The Heart of Spiritual Psychology.* Hay House Inc.

Jalaluddin Mevlana Rumi. 2004 (first published 1273). *The Essential Rumi.* HaperOne.

Joan Borysenko, Ph.D. 1996. *A Woman's Book of Life. The Biology, Psychology, and Spirituality of the Feminine Life Cycle.* Riverhead Books.

John-Roger, D.S.S. 2006. *Fulfilling Your Spiritual Promise.* Mandeville Press

King James Version. *The Holy Bible.* 1998. Human Bible Publishers.

Joseph Campbell. 1991. *Reflections on the Art of Living: A Joseph Campbell Companion.* Harper Collins Book.

Patrick McKeown. 2010. *Always Breathe Correctly to unblock nose, stop coughing, wheezing, breathlessness and to develop a perfect face with straight teeth.* ButeykoClinic.com

Patrick McKeown. 2010. *Buteyko Meets Dr. Mew. Buteyko method for children and teenagers, also featuring guidance from orthodontist Dr. Mew to ensure correct facial development and straight teeth.* ButeykoClinic.com

Prem Baba. 2013. *From Suffering to Joy. The Path of the Heart.* Selectbooks, Inc.

Richard Rudd. 2009. *The Gene Keys. Unlocking the Higher Purpose Hidden In Your DNA.* Gene Keys Publishing

Robert Holden. 2013. *Lovability. Knowing How to Love and Be Loved.* Hay House Inc.

About the Author

Inely Cássia Cesna is a Brazilian-American writer, lawyer, mediator, speaker, and coach. She is the founder of the Institute For Next Level Leadership, offering transformational, cutting-edge programs on inner leadership through the mission of empowering leaders from within. Her work focuses on delivering deeper levels of awareness, awakening, and vision for personal success and collective good.

She holds a Doctorate in Spiritual Sciences, a Masters in Spiritual Psychology, a Certification in Soul-Centered Coaching. In addition, she has expertise in Alternative Dispute Resolution and Success in Leadership and Human

Relationships. She also holds a Masters in Intellectual Property from New Hampshire University School of Law, a Juris Doctor in Law from George Mason University, and a Law Degree from the University of Sao Paulo School of Law in Brazil. She has worked as a corporate lawyer in her early career and volunteered as a mediator for Civil Harassment cases in the Los Angeles Court System. She has recently co-authored and published the book 'Critical Axis: Consciousness of Choice in Times of Change.'

Her most incredible life adventure has been motherhood and marriage. She has been married for almost 20 years and mothered two children. She loves dancing, spending time with family and good friends, caring for pets and plants, reading poetry, listening to music, and walking the beach.

Printed in the United States
by Baker & Taylor Publisher Services